Total Teaching

Raising the achievement of vulnerable groups

Neil MacKay

With best wishes

Neil Mac...

May 2016

SEN Books

Total Teaching
Raising the achievement of vulnerable groups

ISBN: 978 1903842 13 3

Published in UK: 2015

SEN Books
618 Leeds Road
Outwood
Wakefield WF1 2LT
Tel/FAX: 01924 871697
www.senbooks.co.uk

Total Teaching
Raising the achievement of vulnerable groups

Contents

```
======================================
```

**Dedicated to the life and memory of
Lesley Evans, an outstanding teacher
who made a difference**

```
======================================
```

Chapter 1
Setting the Scene

Issue 1: How do we create a classroom climate which raises the achievement of vulnerable students?

"No student left behind" would be my mission statement if ever I ran my own school. To achieve this goal I would employ 'Total Teachers' – teachers who were expert educators in their primary and secondary areas but, above all else, they would have 'just enough' of the skills, knowledge and approaches of a special needs specialist. This would be to ensure that, whenever students are stuck, teachers would have the capacity to take 'classroom action', personalising the lesson just enough to move them forward.

This requires the development of an expertise rarely taught during initial teacher training. Even if it were, when I mention this during professional development training, teachers regularly try to tell me that they do not have the time to gain expertise in a range of diverse learning issues while striving to meet the needs of the rest of the class. There is often an unvoiced belief that, because of Government pressure to continually raise standards, children who learn differently should be the responsibility of someone else – specifically the Special Needs Coordinator or teacher with equivalent responsibility.

In an international climate of high stakes testing, reduced funding, increasingly unhelpful inspection processes and political point scoring over education it is easy to understand why class teachers should wish to share the load. But it is also important to appreciate the implications of failing to notice and adjust to unfulfilled learning needs, these can lead to constant low level disruption, frustrated students and wasted life chances.

In the UK in particular, a teacher's failure to secure achievement for vulnerable groups may also be the difference between being judged as good or outstanding during an inspection. The solution, of course, is to develop Total Teaching skills.

Total Teachers operate in a zone of expertise which touches the learning needs of all students. They use personalised approaches for specific learning needs which are moulded into a core strategy, a holistic approach which helps most individuals without always needing to give individual help. Happily, what often happens is that the strategies and approaches put in place to meet the needs of one individual are beneficial for others, in other words, getting it right for one usually gets it right for all.

As the diagram shows, strategies put in place to address sensory issues for a student who has visual or auditory needs will often touch and benefit those with Austism Spectrum (AS) as well as others without formal labels but who definitely work best in a quiet, well ordered classroom. Students with attentional issues value the structure and sequential processing opportunities preferred by those on the Autism Spectrum while often appreciating the freedom of an open ended format that stimulates dyslexics. Also students with Developmental Coordinational Disorder (DCD) often share the same quirky creativity of dyslexic students and appreciate opportunities to think without boundaries.

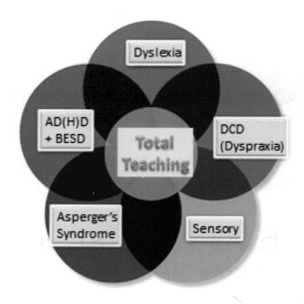

All students can flourish in an environment which pays attention to their sensory needs and also offers a safety net and appropriate scaffolding and frameworks which enable them to structure and organise their thinking. The focus in this book will be on ADHD, Autism Spectrum and Dyslexia.

So the key question is: What do we need to know and be able to do to ensure that we can demonstrate progress in every lesson?

To answer this we need to define the Total Teaching mindset.

Total Teaching mindset: going for the key paradigms

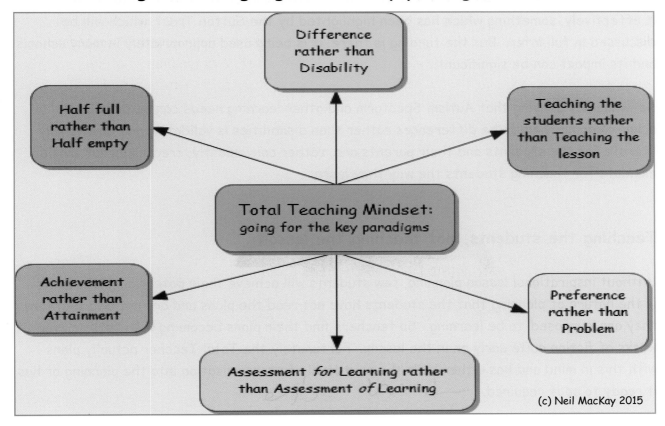

Difference rather than Disability

There seems to be a growing determination around the world to describe and define certain learning issues as disabilities, especially Dyslexia, ADHD and Autism Spectrum. Bearing in mind some well documented benefits conferred by these conditions, which I will discuss in detail later in the book, Total Teachers are likely to share my view that referring to these students as disabled is, at best, unhelpful and, at worst, insulting. There is a serious issue which teachers, especially school leaders, always refer to when I make this point, that until specific needs are officially recognised as disabilities there can be no funding.

This fails to address two important points:

i) Most students who are perceived as needing labels are very unlikely to get them in the current climate. Especially in some countries where it is only possible for a student to get a label if parents can afford a private assessment. Consequently, going down the disability route is actually extremely divisive, actively widening gaps in opportunity caused by socio-economic status.

ii) All schools have funding to respond to the needs of students who are failing to make age appropriate progress, regardless of any label. Indeed, as far as I am aware, this generic pot of money does not require labels to trigger release of funds.

This funding has different names in different countries but the common factor is that its use is at the discretion of the school. Unfortunately not all schools seem to be using it effectively, something which has been highlighted by the Sutton Trust, which will be discussed in full later. But the funding is there, it is being used appropriately in many schools and its impact can be significant.

So, while not denying that Autism Specturm and other learning needs can be disabling, acknowledging them to be differences rather than disabilities is validating and emotionally literate for the students and their parents and, rather conveniently, creates an automatic mandate for teaching students the way they learn.

Teaching the students, not teaching the lesson

Without inspirational lesson planning, few students will achieve their potential. However it is the nature of planning that the students have not read the plans and are not aware of how they are 'supposed' to be learning. So teachers find their plans becoming wish lists or even works of fiction quite early on in the lesson. Fortunately the Total Teacher actually plans with this in mind and has either built the next level of personalisation into the planning or has it ready to go if required.

What typically happens is that one group of students gets the learning point more quickly than anticipated and is ready to move on before the others – this has come as a bit of a surprise because they had struggled in previous lessons and the planning reflected this. Here the teacher scraps the lesson as planned and builds in a degree of personalised 'challenge and stretch' to enable these students to move on. Another group was sailing along in previous lessons and the planning reflects this. However they are currently stuck, this was not anticipated and comes as a surprise to teacher and students alike. Once again the lesson as planned will be scrapped as the teacher personalises it to unpack some issues to enable the students to move forward. A third group appears to have actually read the lesson plan and these students are proceeding as expected, but the teacher is watching them like a hawk, constantly monitoring progress to ensure that the lesson is having enough impact on achievement.

This scenario is being repeated by talented and dedicated teachers on a lesson by lesson basis in classrooms around the world. These teachers are also very tired at the end of the day because of the constant juggling required to meet the diverse learning needs of their students! However this willingness to teach the students rather than the lesson as planned ensures that by the end of the period all students have moved on from their individual starting points. Because our raw material (the students) are very unpredictable – in some cases unstable and potentially volatile – some students will surprise us by sailing through a task and being ready for more much sooner than expected, while others find their task unexpectedly hard and need more support than was planned.

In this situation the best way to ensure disruption is to teach the lesson as planned and to plug on regardless. This temptation may be particularly hard to resist when being observed and especially when the inspectors are in, but, and it is a huge but, it must be resisted at all costs. Few inspectors with any knowledge of teaching would expect to see the lesson taught as planned if it is failing to impact effectively on some individuals. The teacher is more likely to be praised for a flexible response to unexpected needs; though the appropriateness of that actual lesson as planned may, quite rightly, be called into question. The English school inspection process, known as OFSTED, acknowledged a few years ago that the biggest cause of challenging behaviour in a lesson was a teacher's inflexible approach to delivering the curriculum. This is why a core message for Total Teaching is to teach the student not the lesson, but this breaks down when teachers feel pressured to 'cover the curriculum'. Curriculum coverage has nothing to do with teaching and has no place in a Total Teaching classrooom.

> ### The core message for Total Teaching
> ### is to teach the student not the lesson.

There is a healthy tension between the right of access to a national curriculum and having a student's time wasted when a teacher tries to teach something that the students are not yet ready or able to grasp. Teaching reading and spelling in a second language to students who are still trying to acquire basic skills in the first language is a typical example.

I feel strongly that students deserve the opportunity to learn to speak another language – this is a basic right and need in our shrinking global and increasingly multi-cultural world. However I also strongly question the wisdom of trying to teach a completely different orthography on top of one which is already imperfectly grasped. So, personalising the teaching of a Modern Foreign Language to emphasise social usage and marginalise reading and spelling makes sense.

Preference rather than problem

Teaching students the way they prefer to learn almost seems like an over simplification, but the most successful teachers seem to do this automatically. This complements the principle of 'difference not disability' and emphasies the importance of teaching students rather than the lesson. In her work with over 9000 teachers in the USA, Carol Marshall[1] observed that "pupils identified as 'slow' or 'poor' had learning preferences (strengths) not supported within the structures of traditional learning". There is also a growing awareness that a teacher's own preferred way of learning can influence the way s/he teaches, possibly to the detriment of students who have preferences and strengths for other methods.

For example I know that, if I allow my preference for the 'big picture' and my impatience with detail to dominate my planning and teaching, I can leave many students feeling anxious, insecure and under prepared for the task in hand. They need all the detail before they start and prefer a staged and sequential approach with a very clear outcome. So 'teaching students the way I prefer to learn' risks alienating a significant proportion of my class who struggle to learn my way. And, if I am not careful, I can misinterpret their problems and growing disaffection as lack of ability and/or lack of interest. Acknowledging preferences shows respect for individual differences and is an important aspect of Total Teaching. Students have the right to learn in preferred ways and teachers have the responsibility to make this possible, being aware of their own preferences and working to avoid imposing them.

This is reflected in the current commitment in New Zealand to the 'modern learning environment'[2] and more generally in self-directed learning. It is fascinating to observe how many problems apparently associated with Autism Spectrum, ADHD and Dyslexia melt away when students are taught in the ways they prefer to learn. While this is not to deny that, for example, a student's Autism Spectrum can cause problems for the individual and teachers alike, problem solving is an important part of the job we do. So, instead of looking at the sticking points, the Total Teacher should review the learning needs of these individuals and adapt their teaching style to the students' preferred ways of learning.

Now we are recognising the power of individual preferences and giving tacit permission for our students to be themselves. To prefer to work, maybe, in a very logical and sequential way where there are no surprises, everything is cut and dried before starting a task and there is a clearly understood 'exit strategy' that the student can use to be excused from a lesson before overload turns into 'rumble and rage'.

As will be explained later, recognising and personalising for these preferences is not rocket science, and it does go a long way towards securing ability appropriate achievement and attainment while potentially removing some of the pinch points that can cause low level disruption throughout a lesson. However it also needs to be acknowledged in lesson planning that not all students prefer to learn in this way and implications for lesson planning and, in particular, differentiation, will be discussed later.

Assessment for learning rather than assessment of learning

Assessment for learning is formative - it is about monitoring student performance during a lesson and making adjustments as appropriate – basically it helps us teach better.

Assessment of learning is summative - the purpose is to grade students or rank them in some way, typically at the end of a unit or block of instruction. Unfortunately, by the time the assessment is marked the students are usually on to the next unit and it is too late for the data to impact on teaching and learning.

Dr Dylan Wiliam[3] sums it up:

> "Assessment for learning becomes formative assessment only when the
> evidence of student learning is actually used to adapt the teaching work
> to meet student learning needs. If you're not using the evidence to do
> something that you couldn't have done without the evidence, you're not
> doing formative assessment."

The achievement of vulnerable students depends on the ability of teachers to keep track of progress throughout a lesson and to adapt as the lesson unfolds. It all comes back to the willingness and ability to 'notice and adjust'. This is the difference between monitoring the impact of teaching on the learning of an individual or group as the lesson unfolds (Assessment *for* learning) and waiting until books are marked, or even worse, waiting until the end of the topic test has been marked, before recognising mis-matches between intended outcomes and the reality in the classroom (Assessment *of* learning).

In a nutshell, formative assessment for learning usually comes from observation and the use of techniques such as mini white boards, responses to questions, contributions to discussions, 'over the shoulder' marking, etc. and tends not to result in a formal evaluation. Assessment *of* learning tends to result in marks, grades and data and/or the allocation of a level of some sort. This is not to deny the importance of summative assessment as long as it is recognised that the picture it reflects has probably already changed quite dramatically and often for the worse, especially if the problems now identified have not already been addressed throughout the unit or topic. While all students will arguably benefit from top quality assessment for learning, it is the vulnerable learners who have the potential to benefit the most from this fluid and reactive form of assessment and total teaching because, "When implemented well, formative assessment can double the speed of students' learning"[4].

Achievement rather than Attainment

Attainment is a weasel word in education, often being spun to mean whatever is convenient at the time. For our purposes, a level of attainment typically comes from the summative assessment for learning process, usually being expressed as a grade letter or number. The problem with attainment as a measure is that, while it indicates a student's current standing against whatever arbitrary judgment measures are in place, it completely fails to show essential information such as how a student got to this level; how long did it take, is it good enough, and so on. However it is very 'neat and tidy' and so it is much valued as a measure in certain circles.

It is also true that we do not fatten a pig by simply weighing it – the pig needs a stimulating diet if it is to grow. And this is where placing achievement above attainment as a measure of impact and effectiveness is arguably of more value.

In the UK, achievement is generally accepted as being a combination of attainment and progress – identifying where a student currently is (attainment) and looking at starting points and the journeys to where they are now (progress). Progress can be tricky to pin down if a school or individual teacher relies overly on data. But simple measures like comparisons of work samples over a period of time can provide the clearest evidence of progress over time and, of great importance, the impact of the teaching approach, the impact of the phonic programme and so on. So looking at progress alongside attainment gives a much more accurate picture of achievement.

This is especially so for two specific groups to be found in every classroom;

   i) vulnerable students who may not be currently attaining at a high level, but who, because of a very low starting point, are actually making significant progress and so are achieving very well.

   ii) 'flat lining' able students who have been attaining at a high level throughout the year but who have not made any progress in terms of developing new skills and insights and so are not actually achieving.

Identifying and celebrating achievement is a key part of Total Teaching. For some students, chasing age appropriate attainments is an unrealistic goal – consider the number of highly successful dyslexic entreprenuers who failed to achieve even age appropriate reading standards in school yet have gone on to run multi-national companies.

Legendary golfer, Jack Nicklaus[5], defines achievement as being, "largely the product of steadily raising one's levels of aspiration and expectations". This validates the process of identifying and promoting 'baby steps' towards an interim goal, so reinforcing the learner's sense of achievement, self worth and driving the motivation to try even harder.

   Total Teachers need to ask: **"Is my teaching having enough impact on progress?"**

   Or as Professor John Hattie[6] puts it: **"Know thy impact!"**

Half full rather than Half empty

The final mindset is that of positive thinking. I have never met a student who did not want to achieve and attain in school – although I have met plenty who despaired because they felt this was impossible. Recent teaching experience in Australia confirms, once again, that we get what we expect to get from a class. I was modelling inclusive techniques while being observed and was forewarned about the poor behavior and lack of motivation of one of the older, secondary groups. Despite knowing this, I went in with a positive mindset and kept up a fair but challenging pace.

All the while I tried to project my firm belief that the students would be interested in my lesson and be keen to show me what they could do while tactically ignoring much of the 'attitude' coming from the back row. By the end of the lesson all were engaged, even the back row, who had stopped swinging in their chairs, contributing and on task, partly due to carefully chosen activities but due also to the positive atmosphere I worked hard to develop. There is no doubt that had I gone in 'half empty' and looking for trouble, that is exactly what I would have got. Projecting my belief in them and making it possible for them to develop skills and use them in satisfying ways made the difference. But I could not have worked in this way without being able to notice and adjust to a range of social, emotional and cognitive needs as the lesson developed.

Many students who are vulnerable in the school setting share a common trait – they often have sets of skills, talents and abilities that will be of great value in adult life but which are not valued in school. A classic example is the sense of 'rightness' exhibited by some students on the Autism Spectrum. For them it is very much 'my way or the highway'. While this attitude can make them very difficult to teach, it can also be the bedrock of success in later life.

In the words of Venus Williams, a highly successful athlete and entrepreneur who is not best known for her willingness to compromise:

> *"Some people say I have attitude, maybe I do? But I think you have to. You have to believe in yourself when no one else does. That makes you a winner right there."*

So, Total Teaching is about recognising, celebrating and promoting positives, and using current successes to address areas of need.

It is crucial to the future development of vulnerable students to avoid a focus on their deficits. Sadly, there can still be a tendency in some areas to see the student as the major problem, rather than looking at the environment or the instructional practices in the classroom.

The 'half full' approach is built around the cliché that success 'comes in cans rather than cant's' and requires every student to be set up to succeed, to have the opportunity to do something that they are good at in every lesson. Recognising a student's right to be different and personalising teaching to respect this difference is a good starting point.

Monitoring their performance during each task gives immediate feedback to teacher and student, enabling both to fine tune their approaches as a task unfolds, while the focus on step-by-step achievement ensures that the impact of learning is recognised by both parties; analysis of impact is crucial.

Evidence based Total Teaching approaches

Being slow to label

Building on the principle of 'difference, not disability', it seems clear that there is a risk associated with labelling, in terms of stereotyping and reduced expectation. On the other hand, recognising that a student has a learning need and associating that need with a recognised label can be helpful. So perhaps it is reasonable to argue that labels are less of a problem than the people who use them to justify slow progress or behaviour management issues by placing the full burden of failure on the shoulders of the students.

I am going to suggest that labels which carry triggers for progress and attainment may be appropriate in the current climate where growing numbers of students have very clear needs but are unlikely to receive any specialist support. In this context, recognising that a student has clear ADHD type needs should not necessarily limit expectations of behaviour or achievement but rather trigger effective responses which have proved successful with a similar student who actually does have the label.

On balance I feel that labels have a place if they trigger an informed and effective response to an individual's learning needs. But it is also the case that this professional response is the right of all students, with or without labels.

Formative evaluation

Hattie advises teachers to spend more time on formative assessment than on summative. This is about the perceptive teacher monitoring throughout the lesson to make sure that learning is happening – continually asking "Can I see it – is the learning visible?" This fits nicely into the 'notice and adjust' process and also the current trend of setting clear learning outcomes for students. Far better than requiring students to copy learning outcomes from the board is to 'drip feed' them throughout a lesson by asking appropriate questions. My preference is to leave outcomes on the board and invest the time previously spent copying them down to challenging my students to identify where they are in relation to the goal and what they need to do to move on.

Metacognition and 'self-talk'

Metacognition is a complex process which can be summed up as a student knowing how s/he works best and most effectively while performing a task. This 'knowing how' goes hand in hand with allowing alternative evidence of achievement, assessment for learning and the right to work in preferred ways at appropriate times during a lesson.

Evidence based Total Teaching approaches

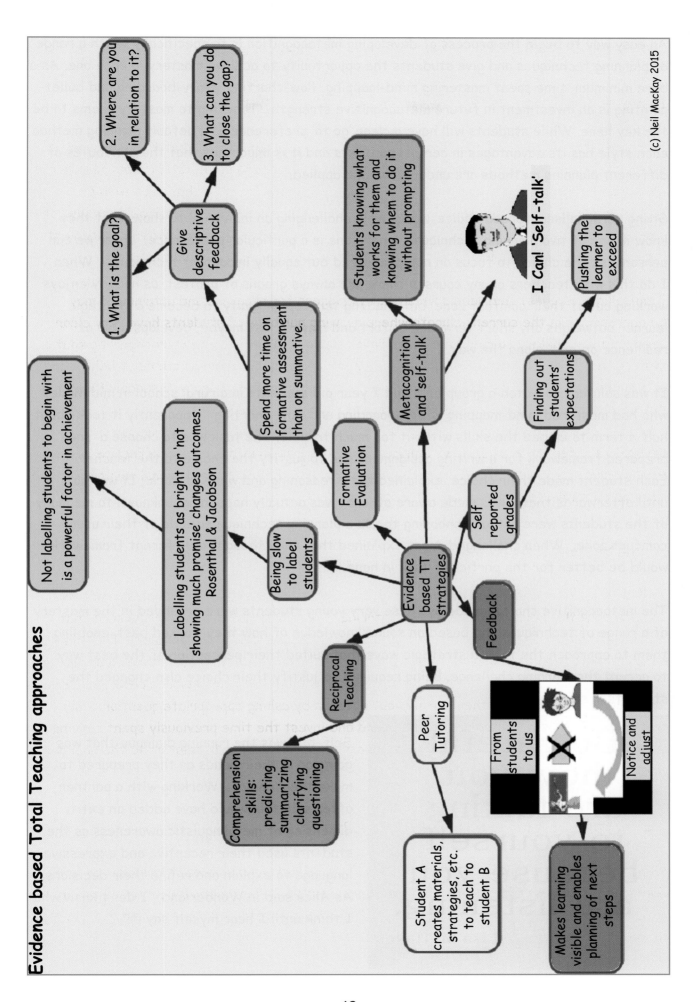

1. What is the goal?

2. Where are you in relation to it?

3. What can you do to close the gap?

Give descriptive feedback

Students knowing what works for them and knowing whem to do it without prompting

I Can! 'Self-talk'

Pushing the learner to exceed

Spend more time on formative assessment than on summative.

Metacognition and 'self-talk'

Finding out students' expectations

Not labelling students to begin with is a powerful factor in achievement

Labelling students as bright or 'not showing much promise' changes outcomes. Rosenthal & Jacobson

Formative Evaluation

Self reported grades

Being slow to label students

Evidence based TT strategies

Feedback

Reciprocal Teaching

Peer Tutoring

From students to us

Notice and adjust

Comprehension skills: predicting summarizing clarifying questioning

Student A creates materials, strategies, etc. to teach to student B

Makes learning visible and enables planning of next steps

An easy way to begin the process of developing metacognition is to specifically teach a range of planning techniques and give students the opportunity to achieve mastery in each one. As a bare minimum, time spent mastering mind-mapping, flow-charting, story-boarding and bullet-pointing is an investment in future metacognitive strength. Teaching to mastery seems to be the key here. While students will have a clear 'go to' preference as a default planning method, each style has its advantages in certain contexts and it is important that the attributes of different planning methods are understood and applied.

Giving personalised 'forced choice' works well, challenging an individual to show what they know in one of two planning techniques, where one is a particular preference. Later we can personalise the choice to focus on non-preferred but equally important techniques. When I do this with teachers on my courses there are always groans of protest, as nobody enjoys working out of their comfort zone, but the long term opportunity to become a strategic learner outweighs any short term discomfort and maybe, just maybe, develops a bit of resilience or 'grit' along the way.

It was salutary to watch a group of 6 and 7 year old students in a rural school in mid-Wales who had mastered mind-mapping, story-boarding and flow-charting. Apparently it took about half a term to embed the skills without too much trouble. The task was to choose a pre-prepared framework for a writing assignment and to justify the choice to the teacher. Each student made their choice, explained their reasoning and went to work. It was not until afterwards that I was made aware of what was actually happening, unknown to me many of the students were actually choosing to use a planning technique outside of their usual comfort zone. When challenged, most explained that they thought a different framework would be better for the particular task in hand.

The metacognitive choices made by these very young students were grounded in the mastery of a range of techniques and based on sound knowledge of how they worked best, enabling them to approach the task in strategic ways that suited their perception of the best way to accept the learning challenge. Being required to justify their choice also engaged the students in self-talk.

> # Be careful how you are talking to yourself because you are listening.
> ~Lisa M. Hayes

Self-talk was the running dialogue that was going on in their heads as they prepared to make their choice. Working with a partner after self-talk would have added an extra dimension of metalinguistic awareness as the students used their receptive and expressive language to explain and refine their decisions. As Alice said in Wonderland, "I don't know what I think until I hear myself say it!"

Harnessing the power of silent thinking enables students and their teachers to make sense of tasks and is arguably under-used in our pressure cooker classrooms. But time to sit back and reflect, especially in a 'no hands up' classroom, gives students the opportunity to work out what they think and where to go next.

Self-questioning is an important part of self-talk and one which also brings in metacognition.

"Is this the best way?"
"Have I made the right choice?"
"Is it working for me at the moment?"
"Will it enable me to meet/beat my goal?"

These methods help the learner develop their metalinguistic awareness when self-questioning uses the thinking out loud strategy. Just asking a student "What are you thinking?" can be a powerful trigger for decision making as by thinking out loud the learner engages in self-talk and tries to make sense of what s/he thinks.

Working in classrooms in South Australia and Manchester recently, I observed students who folded their arms across their chest to show that they were ready to answer a question or had finished work. I was struck by how calm this made the process of thinking and responding, rather than the often intrusive 'hand in the air' which, when accompanied by waving and enthusiastic grunts to attract attention, could be threatening to more reflective students. A compelling video on YouTube, featuring Dylan Wiliam[7], makes the case extremely well and is a good introduction for colleagues who may be sceptical.

How does this look in the classroom?

The key to becoming a total teacher is the acceptance of the preference paradigm, the mind shift that gives students the right to be who they are and to need whatever it is they need in order to learn in their preferred ways.

The shift from viewing current problems as unfulfilled learning preferences places the onus firmly on class teachers to find out what their students are good at and, via 'notice and adjust' responses, to give them opportunities to do more of it. For example, the well documented disparity between ideas and traditional evidence that is arguably the best indicator if Dyslexia becomes a source of frustration for student and teacher alike when the only acceptable way to 'show what you know' is in the form of sentences and paragraphs.

On the other hand alternative evidence of achievement - maybe a mind-map or labelled diagram – will prove that learning is taking place while basic skills are catching up. Some teachers argue that, because this formal style is necessary for national testing and post 16 public exams, it is a waste of time to teach towards anything else but the exams.

However it is only necessary to look at the dismal performance of UK students in international comparison studies to realise how damaging this 'teach to the test' view, with its inevitable consequence of high stakes testing and league tables, is to the future of our children.

On the other hand, identifying an individual's preferred way of learning gives them opportunities to work in personalised ways through a range of alternative evidence approaches. This works particularly well when the techniques are taught to mastery as part of a cross curricular commitment to developing metacognition and developed through differentiation by outcome and task.

Teaching students how to learn is a fundamental part of this process, presenting a range of approaches and giving time to identify what works for them. While supporting students to identify their comfort zones it is also important to push them to develop competencies in other areas so they can take a strategic approach to their learning as required. There will always be times when a flow-chart is better for planning than a mind-map – the trick is to be comfortable with both and choose the appropriate planning technique for the task in hand. So an important attribute of the Total Teacher is a willingness to invest time to build capacity in a variety of ways that may not be obviously related to success in high stakes testing but will lead to an acceleration of learning in the future. By happy coincidence, alternative ways for students to show what they know also form the core of effective assessment for learning so capacity building in one develops expertise in the other.

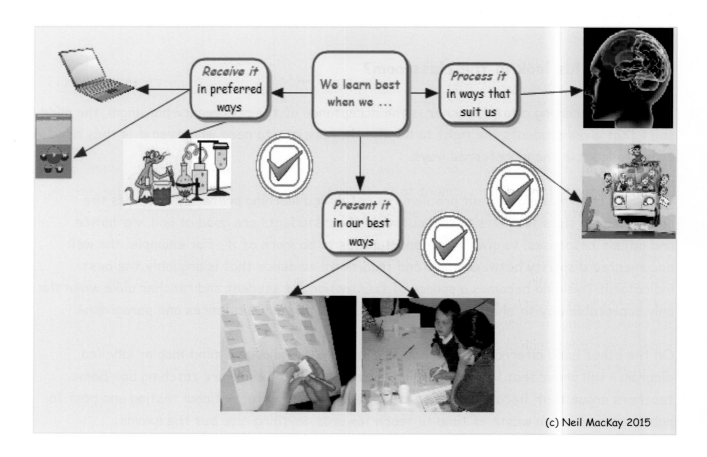

(c) Neil MacKay 2015

The ultimate joy of enabling students to have opportunities in every lesson to be successful and to achieve a learning outcome is that we can 'catch them doing it right' and celebrate their successes. It will be a very jaded (or damaged) student who does not appreciate being told that s/he has done exactly what was being asked of them, especially when the teacher uses the language of success in ways guided by an understanding of the growth mindset, see Chapter 7.

Finding out what our students are good at sets them up to succeed and prepares them to accept ever greater challenges as their competencies and confidence develops. Giving them plenty of opportunities in every lesson to work in their comfort zones and also to be stretched into other ways of working takes learning up to the next level.

We can then turn this on its head to consider students who are not making expected progress, those who are effectively stuck at a point in their education, maybe because they have yet to develop or consolidate the next skill set needed to take them forward. UK inspectors are currently asking "Which students are not benefitting enough from their education?" This assertive question is valuable because it challenges teachers to balance current achievement against expected progress and to focus on what is working for some individuals and, of equal importance, what is not working for others. To put it another way, "Who is not making enough progress over time?"

Relating progress to time is important because, if a student is behind with an aspect of literacy, making 12 months progress in an academic year is not 'enough progress'. The gap has stayed the same. The skills have moved on but the gap has remained the same. According to the latest PIRLS Report[8] England, Australia and New Zealand have up to twice as many students failing to meet the minimum Low Standards as Canada, USA and Singapore. Wheldall et al.[9] argue that the situation in Australia and New Zealand has arisen because of a failure to respond to current research into the importance of basing reading on synthetic phonics.

However, this does not explain the problems in the UK where there has been a Government led and centrally funded commitment to teaching high quality phonics in the primary school. It may be that the consistent under performance of UK students is, in part at least, due to an inspection driven focus on reading levels and accuracy. There is general consensus that the foundation of effective reading and spelling for most students is phonemic awareness, the knowledge of letters and sounds which translates into grapheme/phoneme correspondence. I say 'most' because there are some students who may never acquire automatic phonemic awareness but who will go on to process text effetively in personalised ways. Once phonological awareness begins to develop, students are ready to combine phonics with the whole range of language skills needed to develop fluency and comprehension.

References:

1. Carol Marshall, Teachers' Learning Styles: How they affect student learning
IN: The Clearing House: a Journal of Educational Strategies , Issues and Ideas
Vol. 64, Issue 4 1991
Download from: www.tandfonline.com

2. New Zealand Education, Modern Learning Environment
See: www.minedu.govt.nz/NZEducation/EducationPolicies

3. Dylan Wiliam, Changing Classroom Practice
IN: Educational Leadership, Vol 65, No 4, Dec. 2007 pgs 36-42
Purchase from: www.ascd.org/publications/educational-leadership/dec07

4. Dylan Wiliam, Assessment for Learning: why, what and how?
Cambridge Assessment Network
Download from: www.dylanwiliam.org/Dylan_Wiliams_website/papers

5. Jack Nicklaus, My Story
Simon & Schuster, July 2007

6. John Hattie, In Conversation: Know thy impact
IN: Teaching, Learning and Leading, Spring 2013, Vol. 1 Issue 2.

7. Dylan Wiliam, The Classroom Experiment (Episode 1)
YouTube video

8. Liz Twost, Juliet Sizmur, Shelley Bartlett and Laura Lynn
PIRLS 2001: Reading Achievement in England
NFER, December 2012
Download from: http://www.nfer.ac.uk/publications/PRTZ01/PRTZ01_home.cfm

9. Kevin Wheldall, Robyn Beaman-Wheldall and Jennifer Buckingham
Why Jaydon can't read: the triumph of ideology over evidence in teaching reading
IN: Policy: Vol. 29 No.3, Spring 2013
Downlaod from: www.cis.org.au/images/stories/policy-magazine/2013-spring/29-3-13-jennifer-buckingham.pdf

Chapter 2

Total Teaching and Classroom Action

Effective classroom action is that which has appropriate impact on the achievement of vulnerable learners - it should close the gap between ability and performance. It works well when it is based around the six attributes of the 'good lesson'. But before I look at them it is convenient to focus on the impact of unfulfilled learning needs on the rest of the class.

Dr Steve Chinn talks about 'unproductive classroom behaviours' in his very useful book[1], the graphic below summarises some of Chinn's findings but I have changed the focus to 'priority learners'. This is a phrase in use in New Zealand where it refers to specific groups of students. I have chosen to adopt it as a catch-all phrase for students whose lack of progress is causing concern, regardless of the current levels of achievement, ability and need. A school can identify its own groups of priority learners through monitoring, tracking and interrogation of data and take appropriate action.

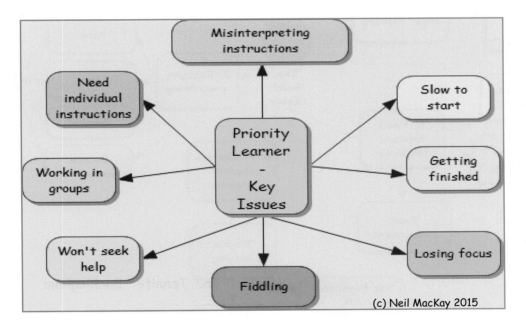

Regardless of the reasons why students engage in unproductive behaviours, the impact on the learning of others can be damaging in the extreme. As Bennett[2] remarks, "low level disruption is like kryptonite for the well-planned lesson". Some examples of low level disruption are presented above and teachers in a number of countries have validated them anecdotally during my workshops. In other words, frustrated students seem to respond to unfulfilled learning needs in the same ways across the world. However, the key issue is less about controlling or managing the behaviours and more about working out why they are happening in the first place.

I am going to present a number of solutions, some evidence based, which epitomise the Total Teaching philosophy, beginning with the criteria of a good lesson. These criteria are an amalgam of best practice from school assessment and quality assurance processes from around the world. Despite differences in culture and emphasis, there is remarkable agreement about the six key elements of a good lesson. They represent a variety of approaches which enable teachers to help individuals without always needing to give individual help.

1. Clear lesson outcomes
2. Engaging methods
3. Engaging questioning
4. Productive student outcomes
5. Feed forward feedback
6. Student voice plenary

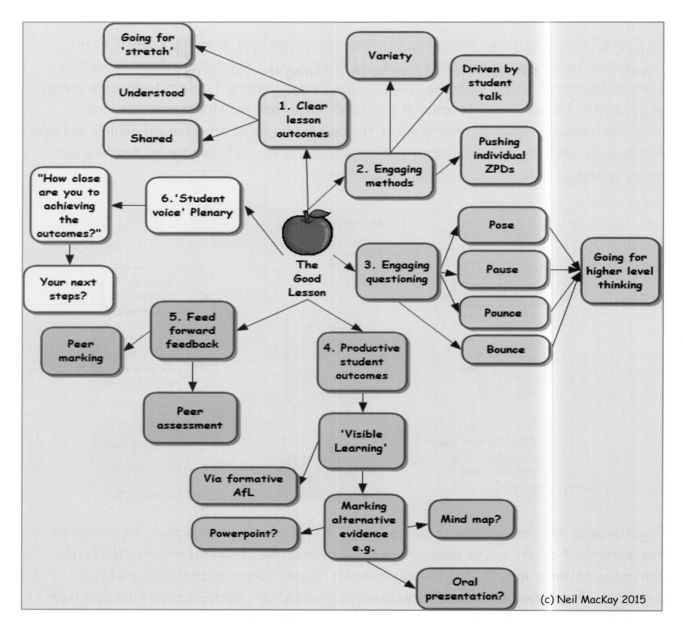

(c) Neil MacKay 2015

When I present this slide in my workshops people regularly challenge me by arguing that this is nothing special because it is 'just' good teaching. While this is undeniably true, it is also true that if we all engaged in good teaching in this way, many special educational needs would become ordinary educational needs and so be met routinely within the classroom.

Total Teaching and the Good Lesson

1. Clear lesson outcomes

There are two main elements that contribute to clear lesson outcomes. They are:

    i) transparent goals
    ii) achievable success criteria

Investing time to make learning goals completely transparent, and personalising them for individuals as appropriate, helps to ensure that students feel able to engage with the task and believe themselves able to meet the goals. Breaking the goals down into a series of achievable success criteria enables students to use metacognition to apply themselves to tasks in ways that suit their learning preferences; lining themselves up against the specific actions necessary to achieve the goals and monitoring their progress through a series of baby steps.

Our unlabelled ASD type students feel reassured by clear lesson outcomes because they know exactly what is required of them and that is what they will deliver – admittedly no more or no less than was asked of them, but they will deliver. Students with the eclectic mindset often associated with Dyslexia and occasionally Dyspraxia tend to use the clarity of the outcomes as a springboard for a more wide-ranging approach. This is, of course, not always appropriate and being aware of this the Total Teacher uses feed forward techniques to rein the students in as necessary and to keep them on track. Clarity also empowers students who struggle to maintain their focus, their attention is often deficient although not necessarily disordered. These students are easily intimidated by complex tasks and quickly revert to unproductive behaviours if they cannot see a way to deliver at an appropriate level. However step-by-step goal setting which is chunked into a series of achievable tasks and supported by regular and rapid formative marking which catches them doing it right, keeps them on track and believing in their ability to achieve the outcome.

2. Engaging methods

Teachers are rightly suspicious of suggestions that they need to be all singing, all dancing for all of the time. But there is little doubt that teachers who have the greatest impact on vulnerable students give freely of their energy and enthusiasm – often to the detriment of their own well-being. If the teacher is excited and enthusiastic it definitely seems to engage the students. Engaging means "tending to draw favourable interest or attention" and few would argue against the need for teaching methods that draw in the interest and attention of our students and a range of these will be discussed later in the book.

For now it is right to emphasise the importance of using strategies that engage the interest and attention of students who, for whatever reason, are close to giving up the struggle to become successful in school. One of the most engaging methods available to the Total Teacher is setting students up to succeed in ways which lead them to believe in their ability. Implicit within this is having a toolkit of methods and approaches to ensure interest through variety. The drilling and repetition necessary to secure automaticity in aspects of phonics can either be deadly or full of stretch and challenge – nothing enlivens potential 'death by phonics' more than a teacher's energy, enthusiasm and sense of fun. Although it has to be said that injections of these elements have to come in from outside most programmes to counteract the 'worthy earnestness' in the language of some manuals. Perhaps one of the key tricks of the trade is to get students interested in their own success. Once this happens they are motivated to pay attention.

Listening to the student voice is an effective way of monitoring the level of engagement. Using plenaries, mini white boards, anonymous post-it responses and a range of assessment for learning approaches enables the Total Teacher to keep tabs on how groups and individuals are feeling about the task in hand and their ability to achieve the learning outcome. Depending on the situation, it also allows for personalisation of the outcome for some students and a challenge to dig deep and crack on for others.

The third strand of engagement is to walk the tightrope that is an individual's zone of proximal development (ZPD) defined by Vigotsky[3] as:

> "functions that have not matured yet, but are in a process of maturing,
> that will mature tomorrow, that are currently in an embryonic state".

Put more simply, it is the difference between what a student can achieve with help, support, differentiation and accommodations and what s/he can achieve unaided. Having earned the trust of pupils by setting them up to succeed, Total Teachers then begin to push harder and harder, driving students into areas of performance and achievement that are almost out of reach – into their ZPDs – but ensuring that there is a safety net to catch them should it be necessary. In my experience the most effective teaching is always on this cusp as, through effective differentiation and scaffolding, students find themselves working far harder than they intended in order to achieve more than they believed possible.

3. Engaging questioning

Questioning techniques which engage the interest of our students are an important part of the Total Teacher's toolkit, especially as many priority learners will be very suspicious of being questioned, seeing this process as yet another potential area for failure and, quite possibly, humiliation. Fear of getting an answer wrong almost always guarantees silence. Having had the opportunity to teach in a number of different countries it is interesting that students all deploy the same tactics when asked a question.

The idea is "How long can we refrain from answering before Mr MacKay cracks and tells us the answer?" Teachers at my workshops often play this game too, with the most determined 'non-answerers' coming from Hong Kong.

The game is called 'The Long Wait' and it works like this:

- The teacher asks a general question and does not get a response
- The teacher asks again – no response
- Time for the long wait – the teacher sits down, gets comfortable, reads a book, does some marking – basically anything but address the question that is on the table
- After an indeterminate period of time the students start to get uneasy and wonder what to do next
- Almost invariably someone remembers the question and – hey presto – we have a discussion

Now is a good time for the teacher to reframe the question without asking for answers, while warning the groups that an answer will be needed shortly. Fear of getting the answer wrong or being put on the spot often resurfaces at this point, especially among smart students with a history of difficulties with basic skills, because at this moment they do not trust their instincts. There are a number of really easy solutions which include:

i) Group answer on a post-it note
ii) Group nominates a spokesperson – this works particularly well when it is made clear that the spokesperson is only the 'voice' of the group and has been told what to say by the group
iii) Teacher nominates a spokesperson – same deal as ii) above
iv) Teacher tunes in to conversations at a distance to catch good answers while walking about, praises the answer and invites the student to share with the group and then the class in a few minutes

This last option is a favourite of mine and rarely lets me down – the students with the good ideas appreciate having them validated by the teacher and having time to prepare before sharing. Occasionally a student prefers not to share and this should be respected. Most will share with their groups and then it is usually possible to get another student to share on behalf of the group. I always keep tabs on my quick thinking, reluctant presenters and work hard to build them up to finally being prepared to share their good ideas.

v) If all else fails try a general request to, "Tell your neighbour"

Pose, Pause, Pounce, Bounce (PPBP)

1. Pose

2. Pause

3. Pounce

4. Bounce

(c) Ross McGill

This is a more structured approach to questioning which has been alive and well in many classrooms, especially in primary schools, for many years. But, because of the potential impact on priority learners, especially those with identifiable but unresolved learning needs, it needs to be part of the toolkit of every teacher. PPPB is an excellent way of teasing out the learning, especially the learning of our 'quick thinking, slow delivering' students. It can also encourage teachers and students to take risks as the technique pushes them into uncharted but exciting territory.

It works like this:

Pose   the teacher poses an 'engaging' question, which is almost invariably open ended. Closed questions, which usually do no more than check understanding or, even worse, remembering what the teacher just said, are rarely engaging.

Lewis Carroll's poem, 'The Jabberwocky' can illustrate the difference between open and closed questions. The teacher reads: "Twas brillig and the slivey toves, did gyre and gimble in the wabe" and asks what the toves were like or what were they doing. These are closed questions which require very low level thinking, really no more than a bit of attention and memory because the answers are on the lines in the text.

Asking "Were the slivey toves right to gyre and gimble?" is an open question requiring deep, off the lines thinking because there is an infinite number of possible answers, none of which are to be found in the poem itself. Engaging questions are challenging, stretching and demand a range of possible answers, all of which could be correct if justified.

Having said this, there is nothing wrong with requiring surface thinking through closed questions, as long as they lead to more interesting questions and answers. Closed questions often work best when asked rhetorically, setting the scene for the deeper thinking open question that is to come.

Pause often for much longer that feels comfortable. Dr Dylan Wiliam quotes a teacher who asks a question and then recites under her breathe "1,2,3,4 got to wait a little more," before even beginning to think about looking for answers. Sometimes the wait time can become excruciatingly long but, in my experience, it is the only way to defeat students who are playing 'The Long Wait' game. Ideally the 'Pause' phase should be a moment of silence, but we all work with students who need to say what has just occurred to them. In this case, it is appropriate to acknowledge the contribution with phrases like "hold that thought". Sometimes it is helpful to write the observation on the board in case the student holding the thought loses it during the PPPB sequence. In my experience many of my students are not slow learners but they are definitely quick forgetters.

Pounce an engaging question has been posed and there has been a pause to gather thoughts and discuss possible answers. In a traditional classroom the next instruction from the teacher is invariably, "Hands up who can......."

In a compelling YouTube video, Dylan Wiliam explains why 'hands down' is a much better option, arguing that it is much better to pounce on students, forcing all to engage in the thinking. He advocates writing names on lolly sticks and drawing them at random which means that all students know they could be put on the spot. In the context of Total Teaching, especially when there is a significant number of students with backgrounds of failure due to unresolved learning needs, my experience suggests that it is better to cushion the 'Pounce' phase using one of the five techniques described earlier.

If the question is worth asking it is probably stretching the ZPD of the students, which implies the possibility of getting it wrong. However, once students realise that, in a Total Teaching classroom there is no failure, only feedback, they are ready for a challenge and may actually be disappointed to miss being pounced on. A neat variation is to pounce on two students, asking one for an answer and the other for a comment/additional views and so on. This allows for a degree of personalisation should a question be at the outer limits of an individual's current level of comfort.

Pouncing for evidence of higher order thinking

Ways to harness Bloom's Taxonomy to support students with weak basic skills to demonstrate their thinking will be discussed later. (See page 73) For now it is sufficient to challenge aspiring Total Teachers to ensure that the questions they use when pouncing inspire higher order thinking rather than just recall and comprehension.

The question stems below demand application, analysis and creativity, requiring students to conceptualise and interact with materials and ideas, rather than reproduce or parrot what they have just read or heard.

What do you think?   What might be?

How might you compare or contrast?   What could you infer?

What is an alternative?   What is your theory about?

Could you invent/compose?   How might you categorise?

The challenging nature of questions based on these stems will engage students who feel safe and who are thus prepared to risk giving an answer that may not be exactly what was expected. However the beauty of phrasing questions in these ways is that the very structure of the language indicates the likelihood of many possible answers. Now we are into the degree of appropriateness, rather than a stark 'right or wrong'.

The Pounce phase can be used to apply healthy pressure as part of a differentiated/ personalised approach. Bouncing it quickly to another student can also work well. When students are ready to be put on the spot, insist that an answer comes from the chosen individual and challenge them to answer as fast as possible. Once we have pounced it helps to maintain the focus on that student, waiting in silence while being prepared to discourage comments, etc. from others. Assuming we get an answer the final phase is to....

Bounce   the answer immediately to another student asking for their opinions. The question stems above work equally well in this context. It is crucial to bounce the answer quickly, whether it is right or wrong, without giving any clues about accuracy or correctness. The question can also be bounced to a group or a sub group in order to engage as many students as possible in the thinking. Dylan Wiliam actually goes as far as to say that students who answer questions develop their IQs more than students who do not, implying that enabling some to answer at the expense of others actually increases the achievement gap – I think he is probably right.

The hardest part of the Bounce phase is holding on to a question which has become a stumbling block. Having the confidence to wait, to unpack without giving anything away while teasing out the reasons behind the thinking makes for a lesson full of stretch and challenge which is difficult to encapsulate in a lesson plan and also to sustain when being observed.

All I can say is that, having undergone Inspector training myself, I believe that any observer who is critical when a lesson follows the students rather than follows the plan in order to get at the learning is not worth listening to, regardless of their position or whatever authority that they may hold. Basically they do not get it! Now, it might be appropriate to ask why the outcome had not been anticipated in the planning, but that is a different question entirely.

4.   Productive student outcomes

Being productive is about working hard to get good results so productive outcomes are about students producing ability appropriate evidence of achievement. The Total Teaching challenge is to get this evidence from students who rarely produce their best in traditional ways – especially through sentences and paragraphs. Asking "How can you show what you know?" is a good starting point because it gives students permission to use metacognition to make their learning visible in non-traditional ways. This approach is embodied by the process of differentiation by outcome, where the class receives the same input but students can choose to show their learning and understanding in a variety of ways, often referred to as alternative evidence of achievement.

There has been criticism of differentiation by outcome in some circles, especially in some university departments running initial teacher training, calling it 'lazy teaching', this misunderstands the amount of effort required to teach mind-mapping, flow-charting, story-boarding, etc. to total mastery in order to empower students to make strategic choices.

The reality is that effective differentiation by outcome, embodied by a willingness to mark a range of alternative evidence alongside the traditional, often shows the gap between a student's raw ability and weak basic skills more effectively than assessments or other data. Formative assessment for learning provides similar evidence and can be used to track the learning as a lesson unfolds.

5.   Feed forward feedback

While students are on task it is important for the teacher to provide regular, and personalised, feed forward feedback, which is about telling students how to make things better rather than how well they have done.   Telling students how well they are doing and challenging them to articulate their next steps to achieve a goal is likely to have far more impact than telling them what they have missed or need to adjust. This is why formative 'over the shoulder' marking tends to have much more impact on performance than collecting books in and writing lengthy comments which are rarely read and even more rarely incorporated into the next piece of work.

A key element is peer marking and feedback. Although peer marking cannot replace the formal marking and grading of work required by national curriculums around the world, it is a powerful stepping stone on the way to gaining understanding of how a student is thinking – this is especially so for the student doing the marking. More than anything else, peer marking forces students to engage critically with lesson outcomes and to articulate them in the form of judgements. This requires high level thinking and the ability to evaluate and analyse.

As Petty[4] observes:

> *"The most important advantage of self-assessment and peer assessment is that it makes students realise that success or failure depends not on talent, luck or ability, but on practice, effort and using the right strategies. This is motivating and empowering."*

Peer marking can also be used to give a grade – this is especially effective when self-marking because it requires students to understand the grading/levelling criteria in order to apply them to their own work. There is a growing awareness that self-reported grades, especially students predicting their own performance, is a remarkably powerful influence on learning.

Time spent finding out how well students expect to do and then pushing and empowering them to exceed their expectations leads them to a more confident view of their ability to learn and achieve. A simple way to do this is to set a test and invite students to predict their score - they record their prediction and then do the test. Assuming that they have been properly prepared for the test, most students will exceed their expectations, some quite significantly. This works especially well with students who have deliberately set their sights too low.

A word to the wise: Asking individuals to share their predictions often shows that some are deliberately setting their sights too low, maybe because of a lack of confidence and maybe to make a gesture.

I used to challenge this and found that the subsequent arguments took the focus away from the imminent assessment. Now I accept all predications at face value and engage in discussion when the test has been marked.

Talking with students who met or beat their prediction is a good starting point and then it is easy to pick up those whose predictions were far too low. Now is the time to discuss reasons for such low expectations and, in teasing them out, to take the opportunity to celebrate the learning and the achievement. It is also time to challenge for a more stretching personal target to be set the next time. This all takes time but, when done during the early part of the academic year, sets the scene for a more positive future.

A word on 'proper preparation' for tests and assessments. Many smart 'priority learners' rarely do themselves justice in assessments because their home situation makes revision very difficult – there just may not be a quiet place to study. Recognising this I have found it helpful to allocate lesson time to prepare and learn for assessment, especially transforming notes into bullet-points, mind-maps, etc. and then use homework as time to review, effectively flipping the classroom.

An open book assessment is also very useful as a formative assessment. Here the students are set very challenging and searching questions, but have their exercise books and files to refer to. Students are warned that copying chunks of notes will be penalised but paraphrasing and re-framing will not. Open book assessments can also be an epiphany for students whose classwork is very poor and who have rejected all pleas to improve. When during the assessment they realise that their notes are not fit for purpose they are much more likely to acknowledge the need to improve.

6. Student voice plenaries

Reminding ourselves of the principle of 'dialogue not monologue' it is important that the plenary is driven by the students rather than the teacher. When Alice was in Wonderland she did not know what she thought until she heard herself say it and our students are often in a similar position in class. A combination of strategies already discussed plus selected assessment for learning approaches can lead students to articulate and consolidate their learning as they explain it to each other.

The teacher can support the process with a couple of supplementary challenges by saying:

"Tell your neighbour:

- How close you think you are to achieving the learning outcome (or your learning outcome if the class outcome has been personalised for an individual)
- What are your next steps in order to completely achieve the outcome"

I have never understood the purpose behind requiring students to copy down lesson outcomes – especially those with very slow handwriting, because copying down 'teacher words' becomes a rote exercise which is bereft of meaning or significance. Talking through the outcome and then writing down the conclusion to the 'Tell your neighbour' activity pulls together all the principles of the 'Good Lesson' into a coherent whole while creating opportunities for some personalised self-directed learning for the next lesson.

The only problem with this approach occurs when a teacher is trying to cover the curriculum rather than lead the students from where they are to where they need to be. In this case it may be difficult to see how to step back from the pressure of the syllabus. However Total Teachers are student focussed rather than syllabus driven so this problem will not occur!

This is what Total Teaching is all about – giving all students access to the teaching they need in the mainstream classroom, with ever more personalised intervention being available, much being provided by the class teacher, as required. This will not work for all of the students for all of the time, although it will help many individuals without giving individual help. When learning issues persist, despite inspired class teaching, there needs to be a series of ever more personalised and 'interventionist' opportunities for supported learning.

Recap

Issue 1 for Total Teaching is:

How do we create a classroom climate which raises the achievement of vulnerable students?

The Total Teaching solution is:

Developing the Total Teaching mindset of 'preference rather than problem'.

by:

- Thinking 'preference' rather than problem, thinking 'difference' rather than disability
- Teaching the students rather than the lesson or the syllabus
- Assessing for learning much more frequently than assessing of learning, - keep it formative
- Being slow to label – keep an open mind
- Finding out what individuals are good at and giving them opportunities to do more
- Demand engagement during discussions – use PPPB
- Organising opportunities for peer marking and peer assessment

References

1. **Steve Chinn,   Addressing the Unproductive Classroom Behaviours of Students with Special Needs** Jessica Kingsley Publishers, 2010

2. **Julie Bennett,   Dyslexia Pocketbook**
2nd Edition, Teachers Pocketbooks, 2013

3. **Lev Vygotsky,   Dinamika umstvennogo razvitiia shkol'nika v sviazi s obucheniem**
IN: Unstvennoe razvitie detei v protsesse obucheniia pp.33-52, Moscow 1935

4. **Geoff Petty,   Evidence Based Teaching: a practical approach**
Nelson Thornes, 2009

Chapter 3

Identifying Learning Needs

Issue 2: How can I identify and meet the specific learning needs of students who are not making progress but do not have labels or support?

Pashler[1] found that students expressed clear preferences about how information should be presented to them, though they varied in the degree to which they had specific aptitudes for different kinds of thinking and processing different kinds of information. But, and it is a hugely significant 'but', they "found virtually no evidence for validating the educational applications of learning styles."

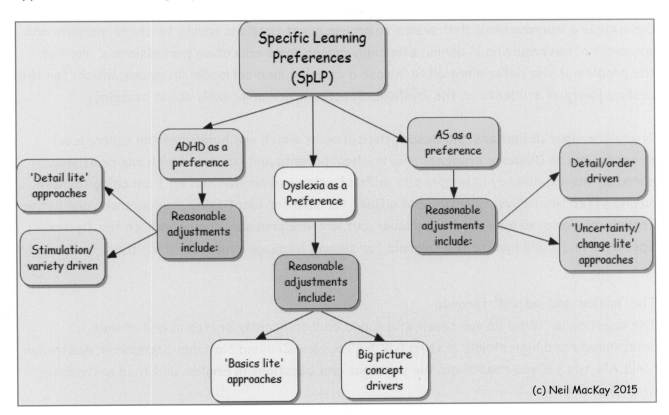

(c) Neil MacKay 2015

Although it seems that fewer and fewer students have formal labels of learning need, most teachers will have come across students with these labels at some time in their career. The Total Teaching focus is on the 15-20% of students in every classroom who do not have labels but have similar types of needs to the handful (typically less than 4%) who have been formally identified as having ADHD, ASD, Dyspraxia or Dyslexia. This is not to deny the importance of meeting the needs of students with the most severe difficulties, rather it is to acknowledge that they will not spend most of their time in the mainstream classroom.

So, regardless of whatever specialist support is available, the impact of such support will be nullified if the generic, day by day learning environment is not appropriate and conducive to preferred ways of learning. This is yet another reason why the Total Teaching paradigm is so important.

Total Teaching and Dyslexia

Introducing Dyslexia as a 'Spectrum Learning Need'

Dyslexia manifests itself in myriad ways in the classroom and the outside world. Students present with a continuum of need, with issues for learning ranging from unexpected difficulties with spelling complex words under pressure to an almost complete inability to link letters with sounds. The notion of Dyslexic needs fitting into a spectrum is being accepted by teachers around the world, it makes sense to them and offers perceptions which are easily transformed into classroom action.

Dyslexia as an 'explanation' rather than a label

Dyslexia is a learning need that seems to arouse great passions among teachers, parents and 'experts', often resulting in denial, especially among some education professionals. Part of the problem is the determination to impose a complex medical model on issues, which, for the vast majority of students on the Dyslexia Spectrum, are principally about pedagogy.

There are many definitions and descriptions, few of which are helpful at the school level or accessible to Dyslexic students and/or their parents and some of which are positively harmful. Having already attempted to define Dyslexia in earlier writing I am going to move on and offer the following 'notice and adjust' formula for identifying students who are native English speakers, who do not have a label, but who are probably somewhere on the Dyslexia Spectrum and I will modify the formula for second language students after that.

The 'notice and adjust' formula

The question is: "Who do you teach who would do significantly better in end of unit assessments and high stakes testing (UK SATS, New Zealand National Standards, Australian NAPLAN, etc.) if you read them the passages and questions in English and then write down what they say?"

I ask this regularly in my workshops and teachers are immediately able to come up with a list of students who have rarely been labelled as Dyslexic. Yet Dyslexia offers a very helpful and logical explanation for the disparity between what they know, understand and can express verbally and what actually comes out on paper, in other words, these students are on the Dyslexia Spectrum.

For obvious reasons, students for whom English is a second or additional language need the reading and scribing done in their home language. The question for this group is: "Who do you teach who do significantly better in end of unit assessments and high stakes testing (UK SATS, New Zealand National Standards, Australian NAPLAN etc) if you read them the passages and questions in their home language and then write down what they say?"

Both processes identify the 'think faster' students who will learn best when taught in ways that reflect their preferences. This will include:

- More time
- Choices of assignment and presentation style
- Much more visual
- More concrete and 'real world'
- Big picture opportunities
- 'Basics lite' - alternative ways to record
- Always establishing context and purpose before reading anything

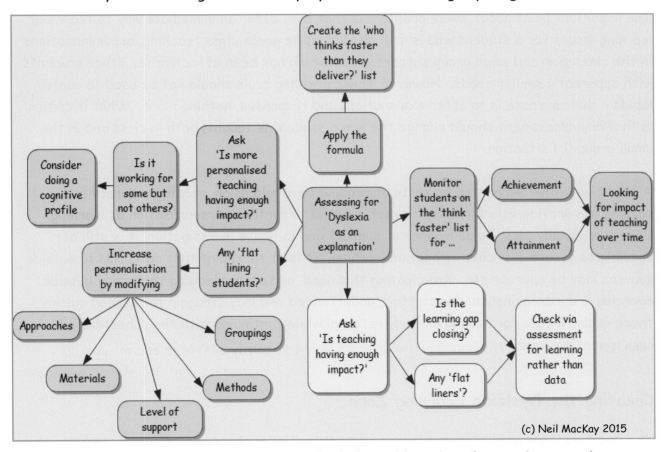

(c) Neil MacKay 2015

Applying the informal screen to create the 'think faster' list identifies students on the Dyslexia Spectrum and facilitates closer monitoring for the impact of slightly more personalised teaching. When, despite this initial level of personalisation, some students continue to 'flat line' the class teacher responds by increased personalisation and more focused monitoring. If this fails to have enough impact on achievement, the next step is a referral to the school's delegated teacher with specific responsibility for coordinating support for vulnerable students.

Using a Cognitive Profiling Tool

In a Total Teaching school there will be a clear policy statement about what accommodations and personalised learning opportunities are to be made available in the classroom when students fail to achieve. So, the first question to be asked of the class teacher is "What have you done already?" Assuming that policy has been followed and there is supporting evidence, the next step is for more in depth investigation of the barriers to learning. One response could be to make a referral to an Educational Psychologist, assuming available funding and being prepared to wait for an appointment. Another response is to purchase a commercial cognitive profiling tool which can be a quick, easy and very professional way to identify issues and next steps.

My current favourites are profilers from the LUCID suite and the Dyslexia Portfolio. Both have strengths and weaknesses, especially in terms of the usual risk of false positives and negatives, but both show patterns of strength and weakness and offer solutions – the LUCID manual is especially good for this.

The important point about these profilers is that they offer an immediate way to tease out learning issues for a student who is still stuck despite great class teaching, accommodations in the classroom and small group support, all of which has been effective for other students with apparently similar needs. However, these profiling tools should not be used to confer labels – their purpose is to offer explanations and responses, nothing more. What is critical is that any assessment should change the way a student is taught, both in class and in the small group/1:1 situation.

A cognitive profile supported by tests of reading comprehension, reading accuracy and spelling will provide valuable insights that can lead to further personalisation of learning. Very occasionally, despite all manner of support and in-house investigation, it is still not possible to secure sufficient impact on learning. It is at this point that referrals to outside sources may be appropriate. Anticipating this need, and acknowledging that many outside agencies are increasingly under staffed, underfunded and may struggle to respond quickly, there is also a case for making an early referral while continuing with the school-based assessment package.

Creating the Dyslexia Learning Zone

The Dyslexia learning preference incurs costs as well as confers opportunities. Hearing the difference between sounds is challenging for many on the Dyslexia Spectrum and is especially significant for students without a label. These students rely on the ability of perceptive class teachers to notice unexpected difficulties in sound/symbol acquisition and to respond appropriately through reasonable adjustments.

While it is perfectly valid to use a phonic programme with such students, their progress needs to be very carefully monitored to ensure that they are making enough progress. If not, the programme needs to be changed very quickly – one size will not fit all and there is no panacea, regardless of rhetoric from certain quarters.

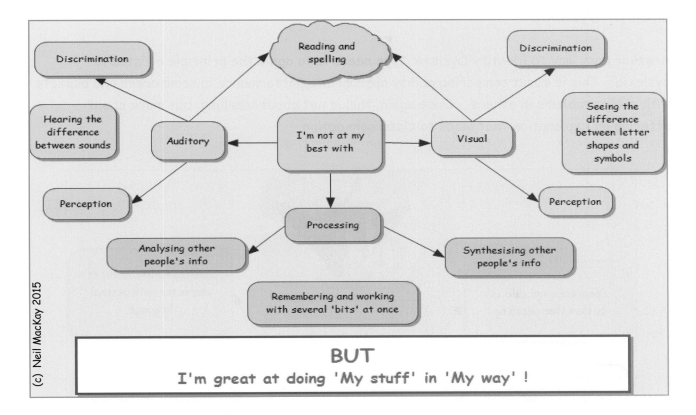

The first step is likely to be a request for a hearing assessment and, while waiting for that to come through, classroom adjustments could include:

- reducing the number of sounds to be learnt in a week
- providing opportunities for over-learning, especially through precision teaching
- going for mastery (80% success) before moving on to a new sound or skill
- creating even more multi-sensory opportunities – the UK Letters and Sounds programme[4] can be especially effective when the sound box activities are completed using plastic letters. This adds that vital extra 'hands on' element which other programmes can marginalise.
- peer support
- support from a Teaching Assistant/Teacher Aide
- evaluating the impact of the current phonic programme and consider more visual whole word/whole language approaches

Another common issue can be recognising the difference between similar shapes and patterns. Problems with b/d reversals, was/saw combinations, etc. are typical of many students on the Dyslexia Spectrum.

Again it is always worth considering a referral to an optometrist while taking immediate action in the form of a visual stress test to establish a possible preference for background colour and using coloured overlays.

Stealth Dyslexia

Another easy way to identify Dyslexic type needs is to apply the principle of 'stealth dyslexia'. This is about comparing ability appropriate performance in some areas and aspects with clear problems in others. Once again, this is not about labelling, but more about offering an explanation that leads to classroom action.

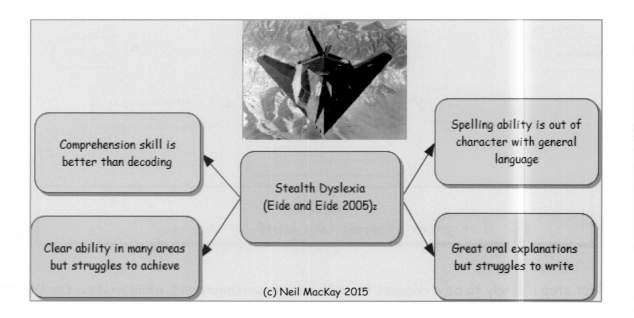

Comprehension skill is better than decoding

Clear ability in many areas but struggles to achieve

Stealth Dyslexia (Eide and Eide 2005)[2]

Spelling ability is out of character with general language

Great oral explanations but struggles to write

(c) Neil MacKay 2015

Dyslexia robs students of time[3] as processing information under pressure of time is often a problem. This is especially the case when the source material has not been properly introduced in terms of context, etc. and issues are often compounded by vulnerable visual and/or auditory processing.

There is also a significant memory component when it comes to recalling and juggling information or concepts across a range of sources, especially when reading is approaching frustration level – notionally when the student makes more than 2 mistakes per 10 words.

Once reading approaches frustration level, and there is really very little margin for error, more and more brainpower is diverted to decoding at the expense of comprehension.

Classroom adjustments, which will be discussed later (see Chapter 9), include:

- paired reading
- reciprocal teaching
- alternative evidence
- marking plans without always requiring them to be written up
- teaching mind-mapping, story-boarding, flow-charting and bullet-pointing to mastery
- kinaesthetic opportunities to sort, sequence and process information

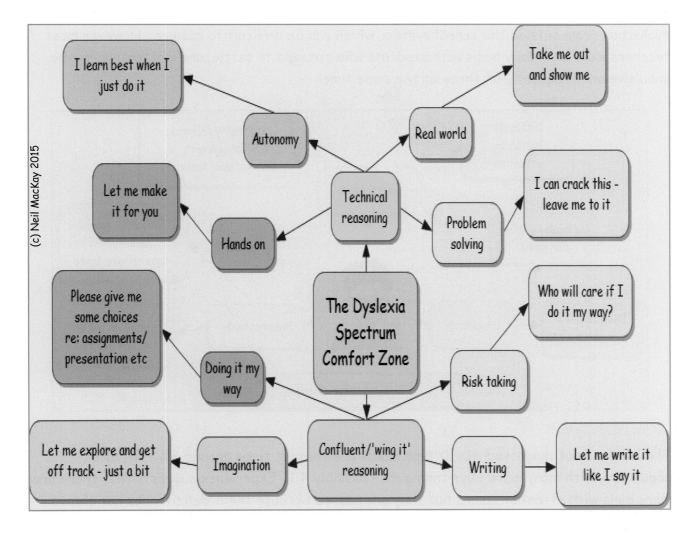

(c) Neil MacKay 2015

The comfort zone for students with Dyslexic type needs is built around a combination of technical (hands on, real life problem solving), confluent (where ideas flow together) and 'wing it' reasoning which centres on a preference for improvisation and figuring things out as s/he goes along.

Students on the Dyslexia Spectrum seem to appreciate opportunities to interact with 'real world' issues in practical and preferential ways and usually value having a choice of assignment.

Students also appreciate a degree of choice in presenting evidence of learning, especially when formative assessment for learning evidence is accepted. Being trained to use a range of frameworks and scaffolds provides a structure for writing which allows imagination and creativity to shine through as does a teacher's acceptance that the final product may be very different from what was initially envisaged.

Total Teaching and ADHD

The official label of an attention deficit, with or without hyperactivity, relies on a medical evaluation from outside the school system, which can be difficult to acquire. However most teachers work on a daily basis with students who struggle to settle, are inattentive, maybe impulsive and frequently all three at the same time!

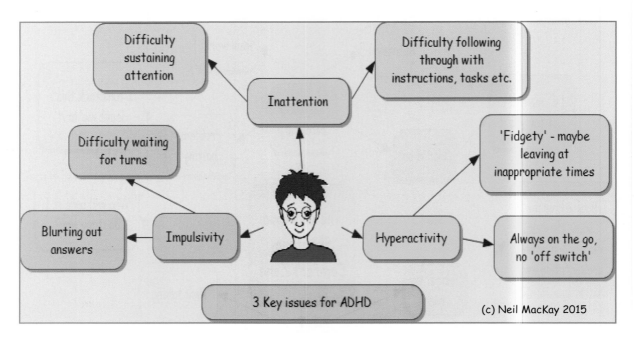

The incidence of diagnosed ADHD type needs are thought to be around 3% - 5% of a population, with many more boys than girls – possibly 4:1. Experience suggests that there are more girls with attention issues but they are missed because their 'deficit' does not always include the easy to spot element of hyperactivity. Leaving aside the relatively small number of students with an official label, the number of students in classes who display the three key issues above seems to be growing almost day by day.

On the other hand it is important to avoid demonising difficult students. I found this mind map recently which purports to identify ADHD in the classroom. It also describes many of the classes I taught as a young teacher. Interestingly the incidence of these types of behaviours reduced dramatically as I gained in experience, suggesting that I was probably the cause of many of these perceived deficits in attention.

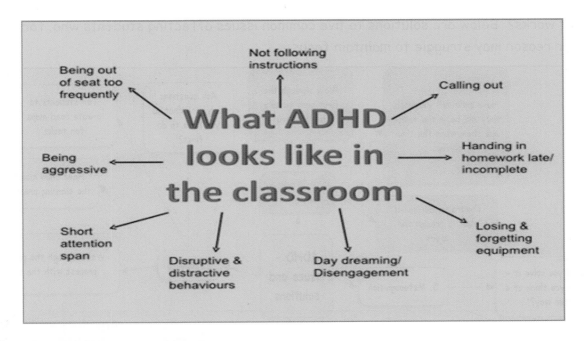

This is not to deny that a very small number of students reacted in this way because they had little choice – they were probably on the ADHD Spectrum. But the rest definitely had a choice, which they exercised by behaving badly when I taught badly and behaving well when I taught well. It may be significant that my ability to engage challenging students seemed to go hand in hand with a growing confidence to gloss over some inappropriate aspects of the curriculum, marginalise others and generally picking and mixing my way through a syllabus. Choosing when to teach my students and when to deliver the curriculum also paid off in terms of exam success due to an investment of time in high tariff core skills and concepts.

There is always a tension between pressure to cover the curriculum and to personalise and differentiate and the current climate may seem to mitigate against this approach. This can be resolved by 'differentiating by depth'. It is essential that all students know about, say, fractions; without this general knowledge they risk a degree of marginalisation. But for some students at a given time in their education it may be enough to leave fractions at the level of sharing bars of chocolate and pizza because they are not ready for addition and subtraction. The key seems to be to use the mandate for differentiation and personalisation to start individuals from where they are in order to ensure achievement in every lesson. Achievement guarantees success and success promotes motivation – it is a win-win situation. But this is unlikely to occur when students are forced to interact with inappropriate learning - that results in frustration and bad behaviour.

As a teacher gains in experience, it is likely that there will be a reduction in ADHD type behaviours for a majority of students. As I learned to recognise ADHD I realised that these students were also managing to hold their behaviour together for longer when I changed the way I was teaching. So, while it might be tempting to say that getting it right for ADHD students gets it right for all, there is also a sense in which getting the classroom learning environment right for all actually gets it right for students with ADHD.

So, what works? Below are solutions to five common issues affecting students who, for whatever reason may struggle to maintain focus.

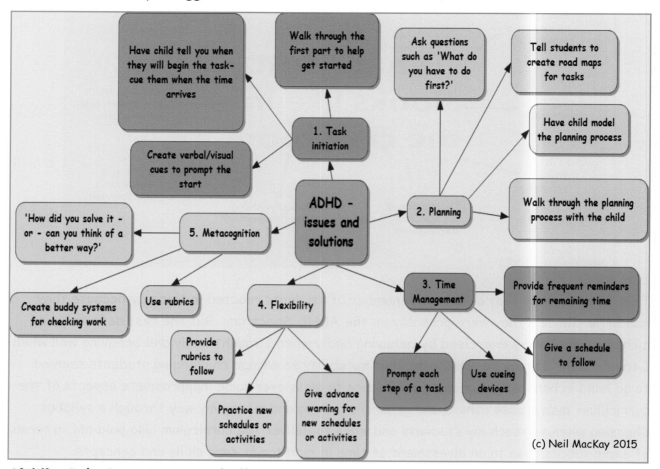

ADHD Solutions in a nutshell

1. Task initiation:

> Full attention before starting linked to a tangible reason why paying attention will be beneficial

2. Planning:

> Plan for a predictable schedule – preferably visible at all times. Checklists work!

3. Time Management:

> Having walked and talked through a stage, warn of imminent changes and cue/prompt as appropriate

4. Flexibility:

> Try a 'forced choice' of rubrics and scaffolds to offer alternative means of recording – "You can either write 2 sides or show me with a mind-map, story-board, flow-chart, etc."

5. Metacognition:

> Make time for 'over the shoulder' marking to give immediate feedback

While these solutions come from hard won personal experience they have been influenced by "50 tips for managing ADHD in the classroom" from the excellent TES Resources[4].

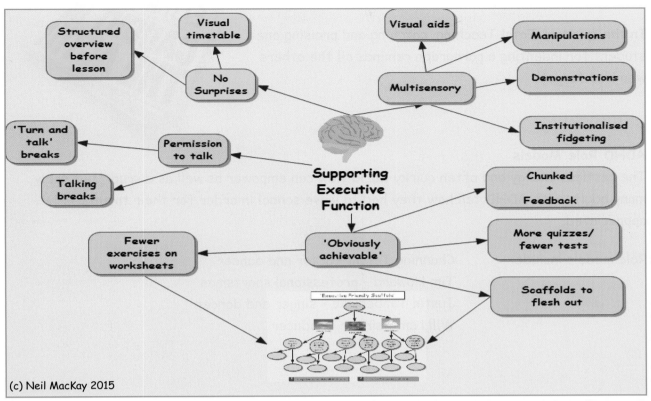

(c) Neil MacKay 2015

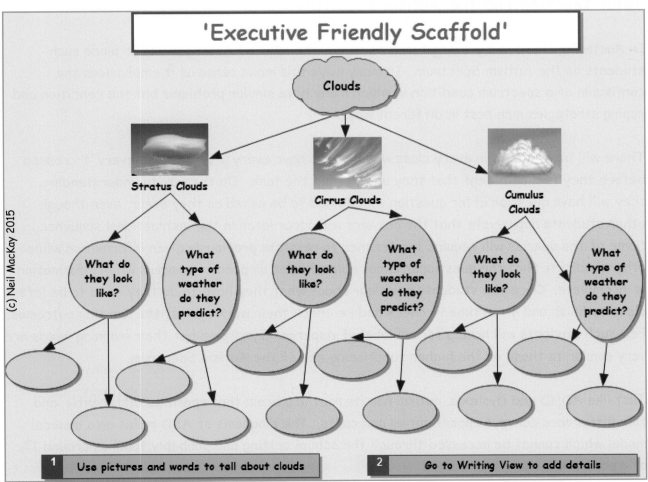

(c) Neil MacKay 2015

The guiding principle: "Set them up to succeed and catch them doing it right." It is all about identifying and celebrating the student of the moment!

In the spirit of Total Teaching, catching and praising one student for indenting a paragraph reminds all the others who also forgot!

ADHD Role Models

The restless energy and often quirky world view can empower as well as disrupt, but sadly, many adults with ADHD tell how they had to leave school in order for their talents to be appreciated.

Role models include:
- Channing Tatum – actor and dancer
- Tim Howard – professional sportsman
- Justin Timberlake – singer and dancer
- Will.i.am – singer, producer

Total Teaching and the Autism Spectrum

In Australia, there is a growing trend to reject the label of Asperger and to place such students on the Autism Spectrum. In many ways this make sense as it emphasises the continuum of a spectrum condition in which many have similar problems but the condition and coping strategies manifest in different ways.

There will be students in every class who need to have every 'i' dotted and every 't' crossed before they feel confident that they understand the task. On the way to understanding, they will have question after question which need to be asked as they occur, even though other students appreciate that the answers will occur later in the instructional sequence. Some of the queries will require the teacher to re-state previously given information while others indicate that the questioner is not able to infer or predict answers when information is incomplete. Once the students are clear about what they have to do they need to be left alone to finish and given time to check and re-check their work against the learning outcomes. Few such students will have a formal label of Asperger Syndrome but their learning needs are very similar to those on the higher functioning end of the Autism Spectrum.

Just like ADHD and Dyslexia, autism has its root in a brain that operates differently, and this difference conveys opportunities and costs. The diagnosis of ASD relies on a medical model which cannot be accessed through the school setting and probably touches around 1% of a population.

Despite the low incidence of formal labels, there is a growing awareness among teachers that more and more students are presenting with 'AS type' learning needs.

Indicators of the AS difference can include:

- Often surprisingly good language – the classic 'little professor'
- Narrow, often all-consuming special interests
- Idiosyncratic learning preferences
- Inflexible approaches to learning, relationships, perceived slights, rules of the game – universal application of rules in all settings
- Often reads fluently with surprisingly poor comprehension – often very similar to second language learners
- Struggles to write fiction but copes better with non-fiction
- Blunt speaking – often unaware of the impact of words on others

Stealth Autism Spectrum

The issues below may help identify a student who will benefit from being taught in an 'Autistic aware' way. As with Dyslexia and ADHD it is important to view the weaknesses in the light of strengths – this reinforces the concept of 'unexpected difficulties in some areas compared with ability appropriate performance in others'.

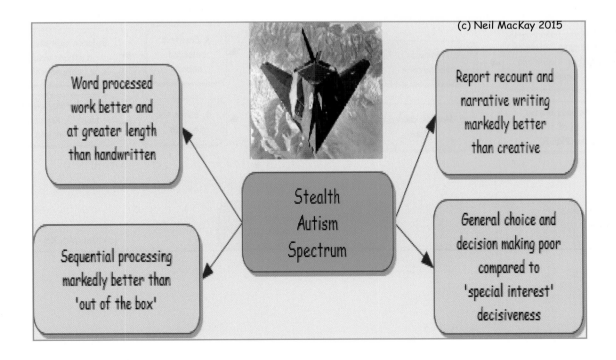

On the other hand, the passionate pursuit of interests, thorough application of rules and principles and blunt speaking, can make an individual very successful in the right job. A touch of Asperger is often the making of a great scientist, mathematician, border guard, traffic warden, school bursar and maybe a successful Headteacher/Principal.

Role models include: Susan Boyle - UK singer

Tim Ellis - Australian magician and author

Adrian Lemo - US hacker

Steve Jobs - Founder of Apple

Classroom Action for AS Learning Needs

A core skill of a Total Teacher is the ability to notice and adjust. Noticing AS type needs carries with it the responsibility to take classroom action to ensure achievement on a lesson-by-lesson basis.

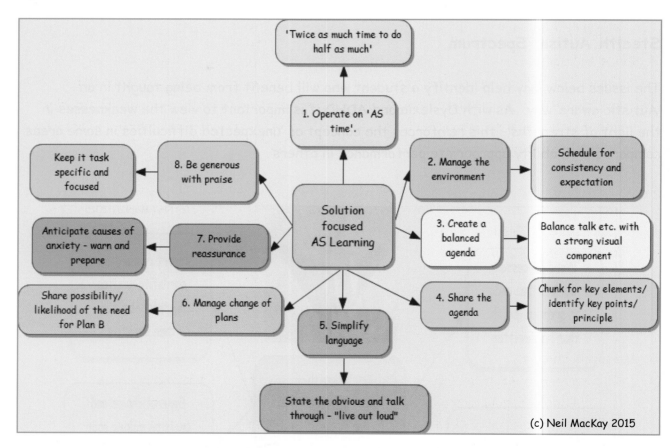

(c) Neil MacKay 2015

AS type solutions in a nutshell

1. AS Learning time:

Plan for more time for students to organise materials, lay them out in an idiosyncratic way, ask exhaustive questions, check every detail, etc. Support by differentiating and personalising tasks and activities.

2. Managing the environment:

Unexpected change causes anxiety, as does not knowing what will happen next. Sharing and planning for the likelihood of change sets expectations and makes uncertainty more manageable.

3. Creating a balanced environment:

The student voice suggests that we need to strike a careful balance between communicating by talk and through other means, especially visual. Therefore, those of us with a tendency to be the 'sage on the stage' need to be aware that, for some students, this is definitely unhelpful. Students on the Autism Spectrum report that a picture, diagram or graphic is worth very many words.

4. Share the agenda:

Careful planning enables teachers to be precise, concise and specific, all elements appreciated by vulnerable students on the Autism Spectrum. Presenting information and instructional sequences in bite size chunks avoids information overload, especially if linked to supporting graphics.

5. Simplify language:

A science teacher once complained to me that his Year 7 students could not look at graphs and 'extrapolate the trend'. However, when I asked them to tell me what might happen next all students responded correctly. As is so often the case, the language was the barrier, not the process. Using subject specific jargon is essential but it must be specifically taught to many students. Assuming they will pick it up by exposure rarely works – specific teaching is required.

6. Managing change:

Students with AS have a strong preference for routine and can find changes challenging. Preparing for change, such as a new timetable, new teacher or even a different classroom by giving plenty of notice and 'counting down' is often helpful, as is taking time to explain the relevance and need for the changes. During the transition period there will be significant anxiety, often manifesting itself in endless questions, often seemingly going over old ground, this is part of the process of assimilation as the student integrates the old with the new. Also it always helps to raise the possibility of the unexpected: fire drills, assemblies, etc., which cannot be anticipated. Finally it may be necessary to point out to colleagues that behavioural issues during times of change are often due to panic and stress rather than making bad choices.

7. Provide reassurance:

The ability to anticipate stress points means that solutions can be built into lesson planning and execution. Try setting a task with a 'health warning'. "I need some creative writing later in the lesson and I know some of us find it tricky. But don't worry, I have a plan and we will make it work." Acknowledging individual preferences can also help: "I cannot avoid talking to you for the next 10 minutes – and I know listening is not everyone's best way. However, here is the mind-map/flow-chart of my key points for each of you. Please listen and use it to add value as I talk."

8. Be generous with praise:

Important though this is, it is essential to be specific and concise about what is being praised, 'gushing' praise is probably worse than useless. However 'growth mindset praise' which is linked to tangibles like motivation, cooperation, perseverance, etc. is effective to reinforce desired behaviour.

As with ADHD, it is hard to beat catching them doing it right. If it is currently impossible to catch them, then it is probably time to consider changing the method, materials, approach, content, grouping, level of support or task.

Autism Spectrum as a preferred way of learning

Below are the main attributes of an 'Autism Aware' learning zone.

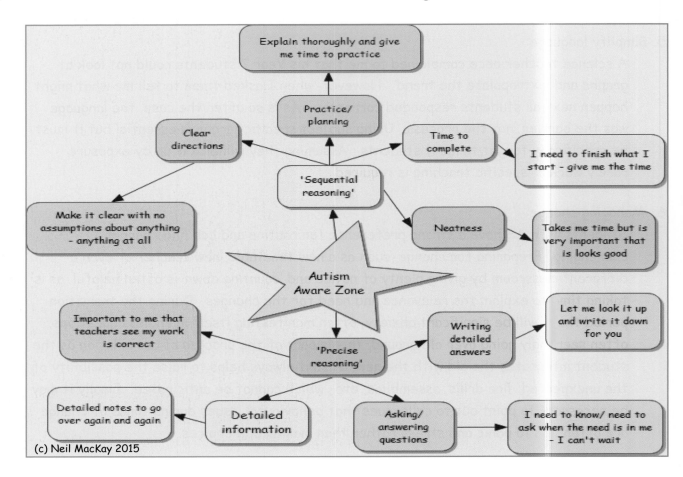

(c) Neil MacKay 2015

When these aspects are in place, they benefit all students who prefer to work in this structured and predictable way. That is not to say that they should not be challenged and pushed into less comfortable zones, of course they must. But it is always easier to cope with less comfortable aspects having come from a place of comfort, security and, above all, success.

Consolidating and stretching the Zones

In some ways the comfort zones for students with Dyslexia and AS needs could be seen as polar opposites, with the ADHD comfort zone being somewhere between the two. There are a number of generic strategies that will be presented shortly. But, before exploring these it is important to discuss the notion of 'zone stretching'. The world outside school can be a very harsh place for young people, especially those who have enjoyed a degree of support throughout school.

Bill Gates is thought to have put it very succinctly in a speech to High School students. in which he set out the 11 rules which are not taught in school. The rule below is especially pertinent in the context of comfort zones.

> **"Rule 8**: *Your school may have done away with winners and losers, but your life* **HAS NOT**. *In some schools they have abolished failing grades and they will give you as* **MANY TIMES** *as you want to get the right answer. This doesn't bear the slightest resemblance to* **ANYTHING IN REAL LIFE"**.[5]
>   *Bill Gates*

So, while being caring and supportive, sheltering students from failure on the road to success, it is also important to acknowledge the reality 'out there'. One step on the road to resilience is to create safe opportunities to work outside of natural comfort zones. By happy chance, the Dyslexia comfort zone is a safe stretch for AS students and vice versa, by an even happier chance, the comfort zone for students on the ADHD spectrum lies between the other two. In challenging students to work in the preferred ways of others makes sense, cuts down planning time and actually works very well. In one sense we already do this in Literacy and Art when we challenge students to write or draw in the style of a famous author, poet or artist.

Now we can challenge students on the Dyslexia Spectrum to work outside of their natural comfort zone and:

- listen to all instructions before starting
- plan carefully
- stick to the plan
- hit an agreed deadline within a specified format

Obviously AS students will be very comfortable when asked to work this way. However, their turn to be stretched will come when they are challenged to:

- make a choice of tasks from a range of options
- 'self start' with limited guidance
- Adapt to new parameters introduced in the middle of a task
- Work towards an open ended outcome

Now students on the Dyslexia Spectrum are feeling very comfortable while those with AS will be feeling quite agitated.

The comfort zone for students on the ADHD Spectrum seems to lie somewhere between the zones for AS and Dyslexia. Students with ADHD type needs seem to work best in a setting which offers:

- choice within structure
- freedom within clear parameters
- clear deadlines with some 'wriggle room'

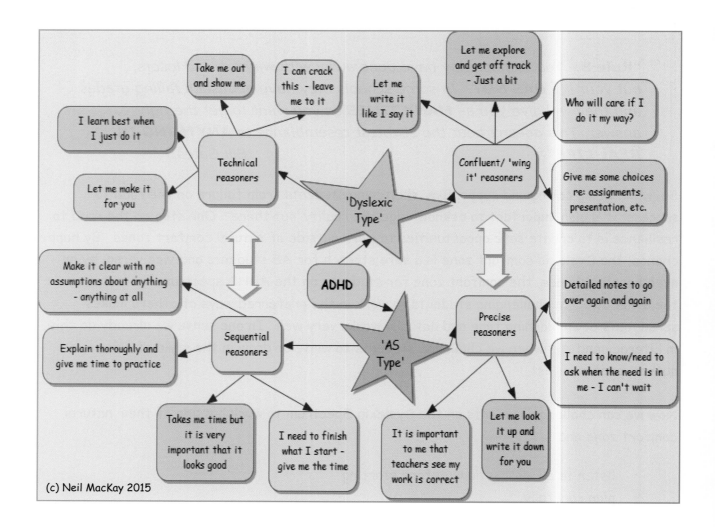

(c) Neil MacKay 2015

The table below pulls the zones into a set of coherent strategies that work across the range of learning needs. These nine strategies are part of the core of Total Teaching.

Working across the Zones	Generic responses to Spectrums
Reducing the load via differentiation and personalisation	'Spectrum times' – twice as long to achieve half as much
Chunking	Clear identification of key points and key principles
Mastery before moving	Students need to be at an 80% success level before moving on
Addressing weaknesses through strengths	Start in a specific comfort zone; work to a level of mastery before stretching
Keep it explicit and episodic	Use scaffolds, frameworks, checklists, visual cues and prompts
Manage time for the students	Talk it through, walk it through – get them to do it as well before starting
Catch them doing it right	Over the shoulder monitoring for Dyslexia and ADHD type students, from a distance monitoring for AS students
Keep it visual for longer	Leave key information on the screen, IWB, etc. so students can refer back
Be generous with praise	Keep it task specific, ensure they link praise with the task

These generic approaches enable Total Teachers to:

- Re-focus the focus to accommodate the ASD spectrum
- Attend to attention to accommodate the ADHD spectrum
- Define the difference to accommodate the SpLD spectrum

Recap

Issue 2 for Total Teaching is:

How can I identify and meet the specific learning needs of students
who are not making progress but do not have labels or support?

The Total Teaching solution is:

To use 'notice and adjust' techniques to identify and promote preferred ways
of learning

by:

- thinking preference not problem, difference not difficulty
- recognising that Dyslexia, Autism and ADHD are spectrum conditions that
  manifest in a wide variety of ways
- using the Learning Zones to personalise and stretch
- teaching a bit less a bit more effectively – using differentiation and
  personalisation to create more time to produce quality work
- actively teaching students in their comfort zones and then going for challenge and
  stretch
- making sure every lesson re-focuses the focus to accommodate the Autism
  Spectrum, attends to attention to accommodate the ADHD Spectrum and defines
  the difference to accommodate the SpLD Spectrum

References

1. Harold Pashler, et al.   Learning Styles: Concepts and Evidence
   IN: Psychological Science in the Public Interest, Vol. 9 No. 3 Dec. 2008
   Download from: http://steinhardtapps.es.its.nyu.edu/create/courses/2174/reading/
        Pashler_et_al_PSPI_9_3.pdf

2. Brock Eide and Fernette Eide, The Dyslexic Advantage:
   Unlocking the hidden potential of the dyslexic brain
   Hay House Publishers, 2011

3. Sally E. Shaywitz,   Overcoming Dyslexia
   Random House, USA, 2005

4. 50 Tips for managing ADD/ADHD in the Classroom
   Download from: https://www.tes.co.uk/teaching-resource

5. Bill Gates, 11 rules you never learn in school
   Download from: http://successogram.com

Chapter 4

Working Memory

Issue 3: My students cannot seem to remember from one moment to the next!

Discussions with teachers during workshops suggest that vulnerable students display very similar behaviours regardless of nationality, socio-economic status, mother tongue, being in selective or non-selective schools, or whether their education is funded by the government/ state or privately in some form of independent, fee-paying institution. Regardless of label or perceived learning need, most students who are struggling seem to behave in similar ways.

While it is easy and perhaps convenient to ascribe these behaviours to problems within a student, many of the issues above could be due to difficulties with remembering instructions, following complex sequences and keeping track of multi-stage tasks. In other words, much of this could be due to problems with memory, specifically working memory. If this is the case, and a growing number of researchers are turning their attention to the issue, then the solution is likely to be based around creating 'memory lite' situations which recognise limitations of working memory and which ensure that students who understand the concepts lesson are properly included, despite struggling with remembering the organisational nuts and bolts.

The brain's post-it note

There seems to be general agreement that working memory can be thought of as the brain's post-it note which is used for a variety of mental jottings, especially "What do I need to do next?" We use these mental jottings or scribbles to remember directions when driving, to purchase those extra items that are not on the shopping list or for that all important phone number. Unfortunately working memory has limited space for storage and processing which can cause problems in daily life. It also presents huge problems in school for many students.

A combination of a lack of processing space and often being under insane pressure of time condemns students to forget instructions. They lose their place when copying from the board or taking dictation, mix up words and the letters within words and generally struggle to 'keep up'. It is too easy to blame the 'unproductive behaviours' overleaf on lack of support, unfulfilled need, lack of motivation, etc. rather than look critically at the memory demands of certain lessons.

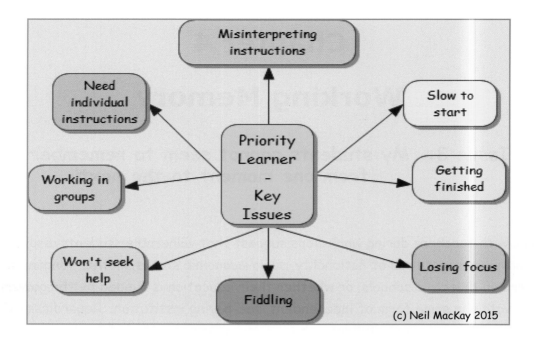

(c) Neil MacKay 2015

The tendency of some students to misinterpret instructions, often despite receiving them individually, can be due to memory overload. Similarly being slow to start, losing focus in the middle of the task and then fiddling instead of getting finished is often the result of forgetting a key part of an instructional sequence.

Problems working in groups, especially a perceived lack of engagement, can be due to losing the thread and preferring not to draw attention to themselves. Finally, students may be reluctant to ask for help if previous experience suggests that they will be criticised for forgetting/not concentrating before help is given.

The profile of a 'Quick Forgetter'

These problems need to be placed in the context of ability appropriate behaviours and performance in certain areas, especially 'special interest' areas.

In these situations a student often performs quite well, which sadly leads to accusations of "S/he can do it when they want to". This is often used as a criticism of the student rather than of boring, over complex lessons where the emphasis is too much on "remember/repeat what you have just been told/just read".

Quick forgetters are rarely at their best in a teaching environment where most questions centre around "guess what the teacher is thinking!" It is also important to acknowledge that the causes of poor working memory seem to have little to do with background, the quality of stimulation at home or pre-school experience.

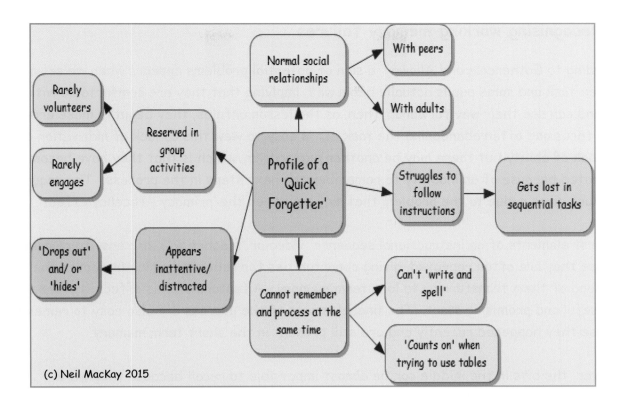

The key factor seems to rest in the power of the frontal lobe. So, professional, educated parents who regularly forget trips or to pick up their children after school are likely to have bequeathed a poorly organised frontal lobe to their children. On the other hand, we have all met students and their parents who come from less favourable backgrounds and who remember everything. In the first instance, the effectiveness of working memory seems to come down to genes. Gathercole and Alloway[1] suggest a seven stage approach to recognising and addressing issues with working memory.

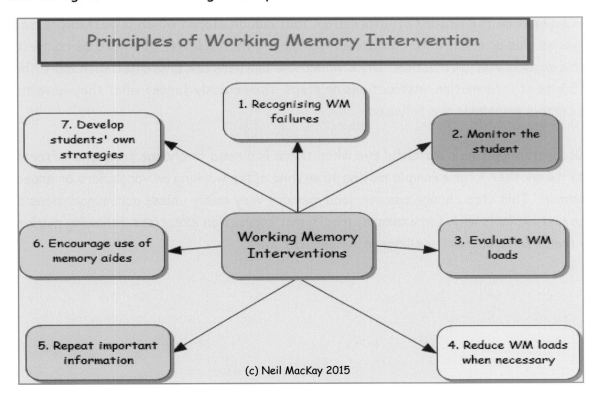

1. Recognising working memory failures

According to Gathercole and Alloway, a sign of potential problems appears when we set a complex task and some pupils actually begin well, implying that they are comfortable with the task and can see their way forward. Then, as the lesson unfolds, they begin to make errors, losing focus and often abandoning the task. It is easy to view this as lack of motivation or even lack of ability but there may be another explanation, which is that they have become frustrated because of an inability to remember the next steps in the process. The sequence of failure gives a clue to the problem that may centre on the 'primacy - recency effect'.

The first elements of an instructional sequence, video or 'teacher talk' are easy to remember because they are often repeated, giving opportunities for rehearsal which increases the likelihood of them transferring to long term memory. A feature of this effect is often a purposeful and promising start. The final elements of the process are also easy to remember because they happened recently and are still present in the short term memory.

However, the bits in the middle can be almost impossible to recall because they were presented too long ago to remain in short term memory and so much has happened since that the learner is overwhelmed. Also a lack of opportunity for rehearsal seems to limit transfer to long term memory which explains why a promising start can quickly dissolve into frustration and apparent lack of motivation. Being aware of the impact of the primacy/recency effect is a good first step in recognising working memory issues.

2. Monitor the student

Monitoring our 'quick forgetters' is important, especially when memory demands are high. There is a limit on the amount of information that can be stored which is best expressed in the '7 items plus or minus 2' rule where an item is one fact, a letter in a word being spelt or part of a sequence of instruction. Once vulnerable learners are presented with more than about 5 bits of information, instructions or steps, they quickly forget what they have to do unless certain principles are followed.

It is also worth keeping a watchful eye when there is a need to change from one 'effortful activity' to another – for example moving to writing after working on vocabulary or aspects of grammar. This step change can overload memory very easily unless accommodations are in place and explains why, for example, traditional 'correction exercises' following marking rarely transfer to correct spellings in subsequent work.

3. Evaluate working memory loads

It is important to identify storage and process demands when planning lessons. Pupils who may be able to recall the stored procedure for doing long division when it is presented as a sum may struggle to remember what to do when the same procedure is presented as a problem. In this instance the extra variable of reading for meaning can prevent access to the stored procedure.

When planning lessons it is helpful to distinguish between what needs to be remembered and what needs to be done. It has already been suggested that pupils who lack the working memory to access stored information and perform complex procedures at the same time will struggle to achieve at ability appropriate levels. However, many common classroom interventions can be fine-tuned to create 'memory lite' situations which reduce storage demands and permit a focus on the process – less 'what' and more 'how'.

The key principles seem to be to ensure that:

- tasks which require significant processing are accommodated, frameworked or scaffolded in some way in order to minimise memory demands
- tasks which require significant demands on memory are structured to require minimal processing, especially during the early stages of learning
- step changes in lessons, when it is necessary to move from one 'effortful activity' to another, are supported by review, explicit guidance in the form of checklists, frameworks and over learning opportunities

Developing the post-it note memory metaphor, it will become obvious that some students have a bigger area on which to record their mental notes than others. At best, working memory seems to struggle when there are more than seven items or chunks and the memory trace begins to decay after 15 – 20 seconds. This has huge implications for the way lessons are planned and delivered. Words like 'because' have 7 letters, making them at the comfortable limit of working memory for many students. Yet a typical word list for 9 year olds in the UK may have polysyllabic words of twice that length. This is where chunking can be effective by breaking complex words into bite sized chunks; 'photosynthesis' has 14 letters but only 5 syllables, so breaking it into syllables reduces memory demands.

Mnemonics

The use of mnemonics is advocated in many well respected phonic schemes and the theory is that learning the mnemonic 'big elephants can understand small elephants' reduces 'because' to 6 memorable chunks. The problem with mnemonics is that the process can actually double the memory load.

The students have to remember the mnemonic, process it to extract the initial sounds and then put the whole thing together to make the word. Teachers often rally to the cause when I express my reservations and cite examples of success. However, I remain unconvinced and have had at least as much success using visual and kinaesthetic approaches. Perhaps it comes down to individual learning preferences? Mnemonics do seem to work well when they are generated and illustrated by the students, this technique builds in an important element of metacognition leading to ownership, which does not happen as easily when s/he is expected to learn something created by someone else. Learning through mnemonics does not seem to be automatically 'memory lite' for all students.

"I can either write or spell – which do you want?"

This actual question from one of my students effectively illustrates how easily working memory can be overloaded, especially when there are weaknesses in certain areas. In this instance, the student recognises that he has enough memory to remember how to spell certain words, but not once he gets into the flow of writing. Once he starts to flow he knows that old, well grooved spelling habits (sed, eny, thay, peple, etc.) will come to the fore as most of his memory will be committed to developing the story line. This also explains why punctuation may also be variable to non-existent.

4. Reduce Working Memory loads

Dividing tasks into 'remembering' and 'doing' is a useful way to evaluate memory demands. At its most simple, doing a task that requires a great deal of memory (remembering to spell, punctuate or use connectives and adjectives while developing an exciting storyline) often means that something has to give. So, it is not unusual for a great storyline with powerful language to come at the expense of spelling and punctuation. When spelling and punctuation has been overly emphasised as a target the opportunity cost is usually the quality of the story, which risks being reduced to the level of, "We went out. Then I died. Then I woke up. It was a dream."

Separating storage and processing

Lesson planning which separates "What do I know?" from "What have I got to do/how do I do it?" is extremely 'memory lite', especially when supported by frameworks, scaffolds, apparatus and kinaesthetic approaches. The example below asks the student to demonstrate understanding of the stages of germination of a seed. In a test situation, this requires the student to access the stored information and sequence it correctly. This sort of task can seriously overload the working memories of some students, setting them up to fail and indicating, sometimes wrongly, that they do not understand the process of germination. One reality is that they do understand but cannot remember. Giving students cards presented at random takes away some of the remembering load and allows a focus on the sequence. For the same reasons, basing correction activities around plastic letter and 'make and break' tasks is similarly effective.

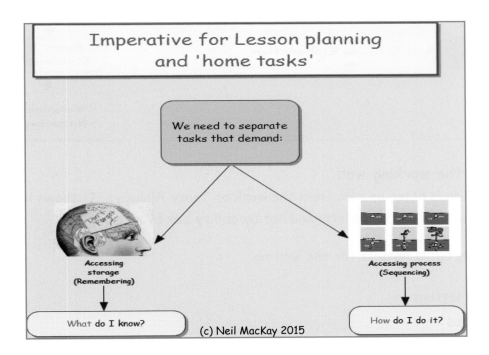

Using checklists and frameworks

There is growing interest in the use of checklists in the classroom. Already used extensively in industry, checklists provide a concrete guide and record of what has happened so far and what is still to be done. The vulnerable working memories of students on the ADHD and Dyslexia Spectrums often operate more effectively when tasks are chunked and ordered in this way. At first sight this does not match their preference for a more eclectic and confluent way of working but they appreciate the quality of the end result. AS Students tend to prefer to work this way anyway.

This framework for persuasive writing is inspired by the work of Sue Palmer[2]. The skeleton is in place, leaving the students with 'headroom' to fill in the gaps without having to worry about what to do next.

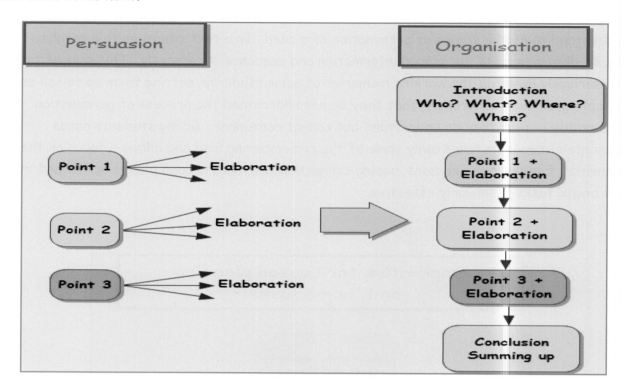

The power of the working wall

The following slide is after an idea from the work of Tracy Alloway[3]. It shows how performance on a task can be determined not by ability but by memory.

The teacher sets out 5 targets for the writing:

- Capital letters
- Full stops
- Wow words
- 'ing' starters (Looking around..)
- 'ly' starters (Suddenly..)

The first student is not especially talented, but has a good working memory. As a result, he will get good marks for being able to remember everything that is required.

The second student forgets to do two of the tasks, despite usually having no problem actually doing them. Marks will be lost as a result.

The third student is a talented writer with a poor working memory, especially for instructional sequences. In this instance, she forgets most of the targets and receives a correspondingly low mark. This mark does not reflect her ability as a writer but it does highlight the vulnerability of her working memory.

How much can a student fit on the 'working memory post-it'?

Don't forget to start each sentence with a Capital letter

Don't forget to start each sentence with a Capital letter and end with a full stop. Can you use and 'wow words'?

Don't forget to start each sentence with a Capital letter and end with a full stop. Can you use and "wow words"? Also can you start a sentence with and 'ing' word or a 'ly' word? More marks if you can!

This student is smart and can do it all, but forgets instructions. Marks will not reflect ability as there is little visible learning. Student is likely to suffer from reduced expectation and frustration.

This student can do the 'in' and 'ly' tasks but forgot to do them. So marks will be okay but not ability appropriate. At risk of coasting as a student.

Plenty of marks just for remembering the task. This student may not be smart but does well because of a good working memory.

Leaving it on the board for longer works

(c) Neil MacKay 2015

After Tracey Packiam Alloway

A simple solution is to find ways to make the targets visible and to keep them visible throughout the task. One obvious way is to ensure that the targets stay on the board or screen, perhaps in a dedicated place, and attention is drawn to them at regular intervals – once is never enough! A more permanent solution is to dedicate part of a working wall with current writing priorities. The working wall can be referred to in every subject in a primary classroom, emphasising the cross-curricular nature of literacy and also providing opportunities for overlearning. This form of targeted semi-permanent display is equally valid in the secondary classroom, especially to emphasise cross-curricular skills.

The framework below offers paragraph starters to shape discursive writing. Discursive writing is a key part of almost every subject in primary and secondary school. But some primary teachers and many secondary teachers lack confidence in the technicalities of the genre. Placing this framework on the wall of every classroom reduces memory demands, provides over learning opportunities and releases working memory to focus on content and concepts rather than structure.

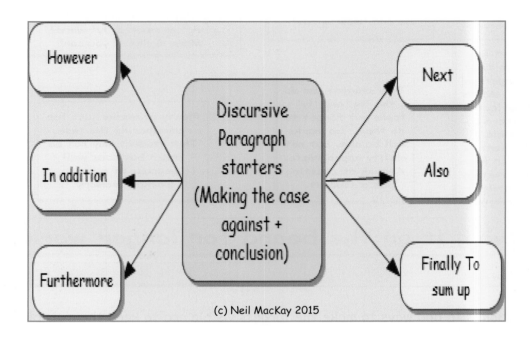

(c) Neil MacKay 2015

'Memory lite' spelling

The seven letters that make up 'because' are on the cusp of effective working memory for many pupils. So pupils who are able to use words like 'temperature', 'environment' and 'prejudice' appropriately in speech but who struggle to spell them correctly in their writing may well be flagging up a memory based encoding difficulty. They know their letters and sounds but are struggling to retrieve them from storage and then process them into the appropriate sequence for spelling, with the same problems occurring in reverse when pupils attempt to break words down into sounds in order to decode them.

Giving pupils the letters needed to spell complex polysyllabic words immediately removes the demand of retrieval from storage – the letters are on the table and ready for use. This way all of a pupil's mental energy can go on processing the sounds into the correct order to make the word. There is also a helpful metacognitive self-checking element – if there are letters left over, they obviously have to go somewhere!

Organising plastic letters into bead boxes placed on every table aids quick letter selection and normalises the process, making it an everyday part of what is done rather than something 'special' for a few. In the picture the pupils are working on their corrections using capital letters because of a windfall gift of thousands of plastic letters – all in capitals.

(c) Neil MacKay 2015

The pupil voice came out positively in favour of capital letters so the school decided to use them. Reducing the number of corrections but requiring them to be learnt with plastic letters is helping these students to lock the words into their long-term memories.

One of the principles of working memory established earlier is the need to chunk items into meaningful groups once the number of items exceeds seven – or fewer in some cases. The use of plastic letters also facilitates chunking when pupils are required to make a word and then break it into syllables. 'Make and break' done in this way adds a kinaesthetic layer to the process. Finding opportunities to turn polysyllabic words into rhythmical chunks also works well when there are tricky digraphs. We can chunk 'Tu-es-day' and 'pe-op-le', while the nine letters of 'beautiful' can become 6 chunks when chanting the names of the first 4 letters, 'b-e-a-u' followed by 'ti-ful'.

Mnemonics also work for some, though it is important to point out that they work best when pupils create their own – learning a teacher's mnemonic often adds another layer of storage and processing which can become self-defeating.

'Memory lite' reading for meaning

Ballpark figures for effective instructional reading tend to centre around 90% accuracy in reading and 80% accuracy in comprehension. Comprehension is about flow, as a pupil gets into the meaning the rate of reading often accelerates as the anticipation of words and phrases takes over from decoding and the text almost becomes one large chunk of meaning. This supports a weak working memory that relies on chunking to compensate for an inability to hold too many items in one go. However, the common practice of drilling pupils to sound out a word when stuck arguably negates this process. It destroys flow, overloads storage and processing as the student attempts to retrieve the sounds from his/her memory and process them to form the word.

Going for 'contextualised guessing'

However the simple mantra "if in doubt leave it out and read to the next full stop" maintains the flow and the integrity of the chunk of text and fits well with current thinking on ways to support a weak working memory. This simple strategy optimises comprehension and facilitates 'contextualised guessing' in order to make sense of the sentence. This will not always work and it is essential pupils have sound word attack skills in their repertoire and the metacognition to use them when the guessed word does not make sense. But the key is knowing when to use word attack skills rather than using them automatically whenever stuck. Another benefit of going for flow is that a problem word may not need sounding out in its entirety, often the first few sounds are enough to trigger the word, because context reduces and defines possible choices. Also ensuring that all possible contextual clues (title, captions, picture, etc.) are explored before beginning to read will enhance processing and reduce the need to go into storage when confronted by an unknown word.

Memory lite Assessment for Learning

Failing to build in opportunities to re-visit, review and consolidate will significantly affect the impact of teaching for a majority of pupils as retention rates fall to around 58% within 20 minutes. Pupils with poor working memories are particularly vulnerable to the Ebbinghaus Forgetting Curve, which demonstrates the dangers of becoming obsessed with pace and coverage at the expense of opportunities for review and revision.

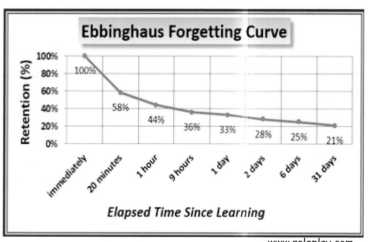

www.roleplay.com

While the expectation from OFSTED is that lessons will have 'appropriate pace' this can be misinterpreted to suggest that what is required is non-stop turbo-charged delivery from the 'sage on the stage'. On the other hand, lessons built around 'spaced review', ideally through a series of assessment for learning activities (AfL), is a perfect fit for pupils with poor working memories. Here a chunk of learning is reviewed and reprised before moving on, keeping the learning uppermost, reducing storage demands and enabling a focus on the task or process in hand.

It is difficult to overstate the power of formative assessment. Dylan Wiliam suggests that,

> "when implemented well, formative assessment can double the speed of students' learning".

Yet the very process of formative assessment depends of stopping the flow in order to review and regroup and should have a negative impact on an already suspect working memory.

Fortunately, the reality is very different and the chunked lesson gives phased opportunities for reflection, discussion, re-framing and the creation of long term memories. A lesson built around a series of spaced reviews ensures that learning is organised into bite sized chunks, each of which is consolidated by review/reprise activities before moving on. Each review has the effect of gradually flattening the forgetting curve as knowledge and skills are re-visited throughout the lesson. This ensures that, after several reviews, much of the learning is locked into long term memory.

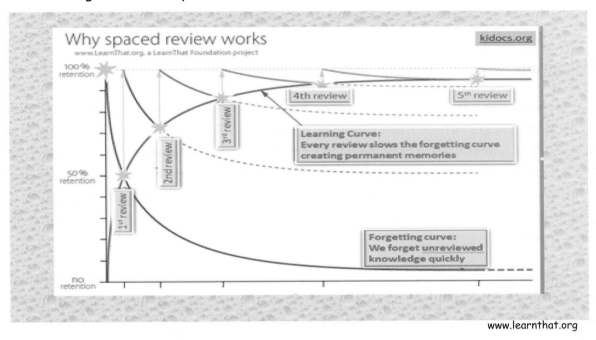

www.learnthat.org

Simple AfL opportunities such as 'Pair share into group share' or '3 key points on your mini white board' offer effective review opportunities which keep the learning uppermost as the lesson unfolds.

5. Repeat important information

A willingness to repeat information on request is a core attribute of a Total Teacher. It is interesting to speculate on how many unproductive behaviours stem from a reluctance to ask for help or clarification, especially if responses to previous requests have been with 'attitude' from the teacher. While I will be the first to acknowledge that some students do not listen and others do not always help themselves, I have learned that it is better to give information, guidance and advice with good grace, as soon as it is requested.

This should not be construed as 'weak teaching'. Rather it is about giving students what is required to move on, getting them going and then having a quiet word in due course about approaches to learning and personal responsibility. Aggressive or emotional responses to requests for repetition or clarification send a very clear message to all students that, in this class, it is best not to ask for help. Creating a climate of "It is ok to ask" is critical, responding to requests for clarification with a smile and "Thanks for asking" encourages pupils to ask for help and goes a long way towards the effective management of behaviour.

It is arguably much better to repeat when asked rather than deal with 'off task' problems later in the lesson. Focussing the attention of pupils with vulnerable memories is also effective. Challenges like, "Paul, get ready to explain to your partner/your group/to me", work well as does a simple, "Rashid, your question coming up next".

This is where PPPB can be so effective. Working walls, frameworks, scaffolds, examples from another group and other devices can be used to anticipate potential sticking points. Once again, these devices help individuals without always needing to give individual help.

6. Encourage use of memory aides

Most busy people use lists to make sure everything gets done while pilots and surgeons rely on extensive checklists rather than depending on memory. Providing simple checklists/to do lists for pupils is a first step in building habits for the future. The next step is supporting them to create their own checklists and rubrics followed by opportunities to evaluate impact and effectiveness. A well planned working wall can be a powerful memory aid, especially when pupils are specifically taught where information is located and how to use the room to overcome problems.

Many secondary schools and a growing number of primary schools encourage the use of mobile phones as memory aides. Making a voice recording of the details and taking a photo of the task on the board ensures that pupils arrive home with a clear idea of what they have to do and a meaningful record from which to refer. Siri is a useful app which allows students to send messages, schedule meetings, make phone calls and more using voice commands.

www.livescribe.com/uk

The livescribe smart pen, allows students to take notes and draw diagrams using a special pen which also records the teacher's voice. When the student places the pen on a note, or maybe a diagram, bullet point, etc. the pen plays back what the teacher was saying at that time. The notes can also be downloaded onto a laptop and be printed. This is a very 'memory lite' option because it allows students to listen and take skeleton notes in any preferred way, in the certain knowledge that there is a recording of the lesson to play back as required.

Low tech and much less expensive solutions are talking tins and talking pegs. Talking Tins provide a simple way of recording and playing back short audio recordings. They can be used by practitioners to record instructions or to scaffold support for key tasks. The red tin can store up to 40 seconds of recorded information.

www.sensetoys.com

Talking pegs work in the same way, storing up to 10 seconds of information or commentary, and are perfect for short instructions and also for showcasing work.

www.tts-group.com

7. Develop students' own strategies: going for metacognition

Learning how to learn - giving opportunities to experiment with a range of ways to remember and process can work really well. Developing a metacognitive awareness and belief in what works is a vital step in becoming a self directed learner.

It could be as simple as giving individuals the opportunity to process information in a variety of ways as an aid to planning and memory. This leads nicely into opportunites to acknowledge both vulnerabilities and preferences by differentiating by outcome, for example, inviting pupils to present their work as bullet-points or a mind-map rather than in sentences may leave more 'head room' to remember details.

Many AfL techniques will provide alternative evidence of achievement and can be used to track learning as a lesson unfolds, enabling teachers to demonstrate the impact of their teaching with potentially vulnerable students.

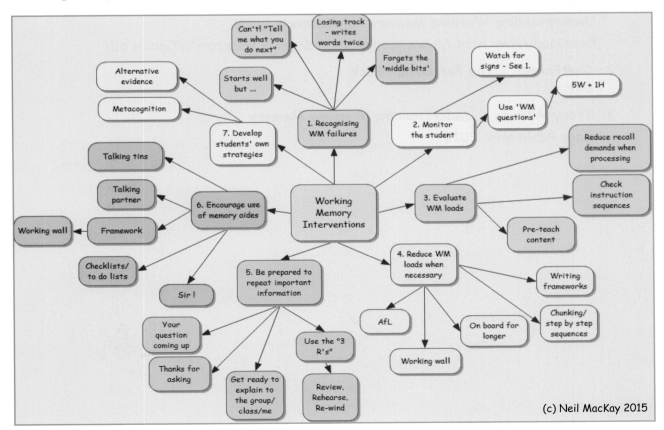

(c) Neil MacKay 2015

Recap

Issue 3 for Total Teaching is:

My students cannot remember from one moment to the next

The Total Teaching solution is:

**To create the 'memory lite' classroom by analysing
and personalising the memory demands in lessons**

by:

- Recognising working memory failures
- Monitoring and evaluating working memory loads
- Reducing memory loads by separating processing and storage tasks
- Being prepared to repeat information and encourage the use of memory aides
- Specifically teaching strategies that students can develop, practice and make their own

References:

1. **Susan E Gathercole and Tracy Alloway**
   Understanding Working Memory: a classroom guide
   Download from: http://www.york.ac.uk/res/wml/Classroom%20guide.pdf

2. **Sue Palmer, The Persuation Book**
   Ginn

3. **Tracy Alloway, Understanding Working Memory**
   Sage Publishers, 2014

Chapter 5

Tracking Progress

Issue 4: How do I keep track of quick thinking, slow delivering students in a busy classroom?

Total Teaching and Assessment for Learning

There is a growing awareness of the importance of monitoring learning throughout a lesson through the planned process of assessment for learning (AfL). A recent study in the UK into excellent practice in primary schools found that teachers in excellent schools were especially good at:

"ensuring that Assessment for Learning was part of lessons and providing sufficient opportunities for children to reflect on their learning".[1]

This excellent practice is very much in the spirit of Total Teaching since it helps and supports individuals without always needing to give individual help.

It is important to distinguish between assessment *for* learning which samples the learning of the whole class, groups and/or individuals as the lesson unfolds, and assessment *of* learning which typically takes place at the end of a block of teaching, end of unit, etc. While both have their place, the opportunities presented by effective AfL are especially important to priority learners. The process enables teachers to monitor learning during the lesson, to quickly identify sticking points and to personalise as appropriate, basically to 'notice and adjust' as the lesson unfolds. And, as is so often the case, measures put in place to support vulnerable groups will have a positive impact on the learning of all students.

There appear to be five main elements:

1. Clear success criteria which are unpacked and understood
2. Discussions, questions and short activities that provide 'visible evidence' of learning
3. 'Feed forward' feedback that enables learners to identify their next steps
4. Empowering students to be in charge of their own learning
5. Harnessing the power of peer tutoring, students as 'instructional resources' for each other

This process can be summed up as feedback, that is feedback to the students about how their learning is going and to the teacher about how well s/he is doing. The importance of feedback has been demonstrated by the Sutton Trust[2], which reported "High impact for low cost, based on moderate evidence", where moderate evidence is defined as "Two or more rigorous meta-analyses of experimental studies of school age students with cognitive or curriculum outcome measures".

This finding is mirrored by Hattie[3] in his work on visible learning which is also based on meta-analyses. Hattie found the most powerful single influence enhancing achievement to be feedback, which has the greatest effect when teachers receive more and better feedback about their teaching.

Note, the word 'receive' – the impact Hattie identified depends on teachers being receptive and responsive to cues from their students as well as being able to tell them how they are doing. Then the "ripple effect back to the student is high". So we are back to finding ways to enable teachers to notice the impact of their teaching on the learning of individuals and then making appropriate adjustments to ensure that the process continues in an upward trajectory for all.

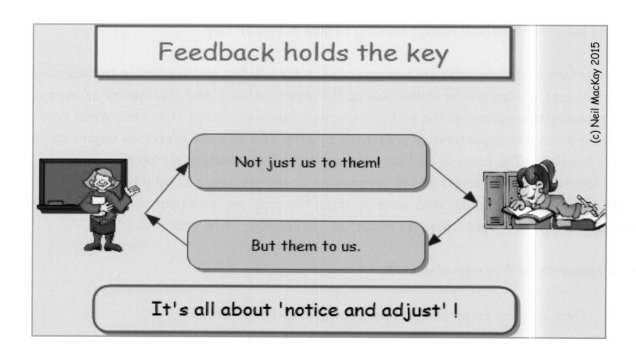

1. Clear success criteria which are unpacked and understood

Regardless of the topic, it is essential that students know what they are learning, why they are learning it, where it fits in with previous learning and how they will know when they have been successful. Most teachers seek to achieve this by writing lesson outcomes or objectives on the board and, in many schools, it is policy for students to copy these goals into their books before the lesson begins. For priority learners, many of whom have slow handwriting and a poor short-term memory, this initial copying task is the first nail in the coffin of yet another lesson struggling to keep up – they are behind before they start and things can only get worse! An easy way to validate their growing sense of frustration is to require them to copy generic, and therefore unachievable, success criteria as well. That is tantamount to lighting the blue touch paper - stand well back!

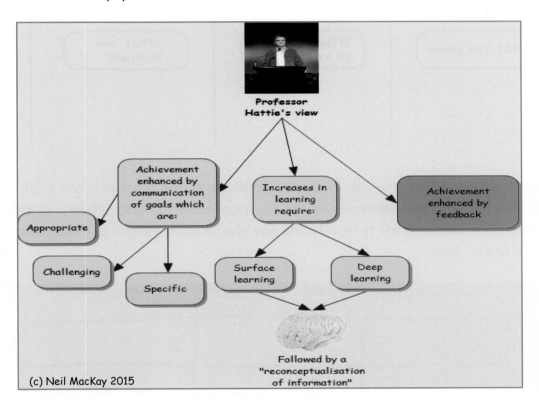

(c) Neil MacKay 2015

A very pragmatic solution is to print title, date, outcomes and, if appropriate, personalised success criteria on strips of paper, which can be stuck into books, enabling students to be ready to go as soon as the learning starts.

A word to the wise: The rest of the class will probably ask why they cannot have the pre-printed strips as well. Unfortunately, I do not have an answer to that because I can see no value in slowing the pace of a lesson down with copying during that critical 'first 5 minutes' when students are especially receptive and ready to learn.

The problem with any form of copying is that it is passive – it does not engage the brain in any way. During this sterile part of the lesson most students will copy quickly and then dismiss while priority learners will copy slowly and then forget – either way both groups will be little wiser about the lesson purpose and direction.

On the other hand, presenting the outcomes on the board and going for a round of 'Tell your neighbour' – initially what we did last lesson and then followed by "How do you think this fits in?" or "What do we need to do/be able to do to move forward?" Snapping from a paired task to 'Tell the table' widens the discussion and a version of a KWL table helps students interact with outcomes and success criteria in meaningful ways.

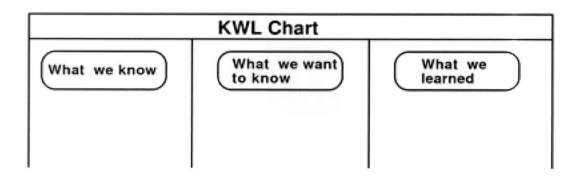

The completed table below provides invaluable feedback to the teacher about prior learning and about how much is remembered from the previous lesson. It also offers a wealth of other information that is likely to modify the way the lesson is taught to individuals, groups or even the whole class.

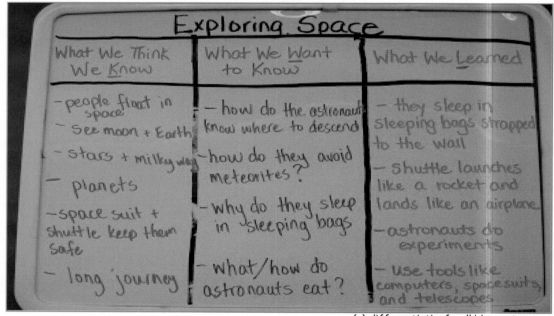

When I present these ideas during workshops, I often hear muttering: "I haven't got time to do this – I need to start teaching". The reality is that, while there may not have been too much actual 'teaching' going on, the learning has already started .

In this scenario the teacher's energy and expertise has gone into creating conditions for learning rather than trying to do the learning for the students. Now we can ask the students to re-frame the success criteria in ways that are meaningful to them and it is time to start teaching. The beauty of working this way is that the learning starts well before any teaching can begin, engaging vulnerable students from the outset and potentially minimising confusion, frustration, disruption, etc. and it need only take a couple of minutes.

2. Discussions, questions and short activities that provide 'visible evidence' of learning

So, the lesson outcomes are understood and unpacked, the success criteria are explicit and we are only 5 minutes into the lesson – what next?

> *"The central idea is that we should use assessment to influence learning and that the teaching should be contingent on what students have learnt, so that while we're teaching we collect evidence about where the students are to make adjustments to our teaching to better meet our students' learning needs".[4]*

Effective AfL provides teachers and students with this visible learning and there is a range of activities that can do the job. Through TES Resources it is possible to download a superb range of assessment for learning activities which will work in most lessons for most age groups. The examples used below are from the 'AfL Toolkit' from the work of Mike Gershon that can also be accessed through his very comprehensive and useful website[5].

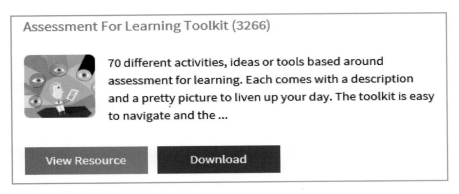

Assessment For Learning Toolkit (3266)

70 different activities, ideas or tools based around assessment for learning. Each comes with a description and a pretty picture to liven up your day. The toolkit is easy to navigate and the ...

View Resource   Download

I have taken some of these ideas and added a Total Teaching perspective, tweaking them to meet the needs of students who think faster than they deliver and who may struggle to demonstrate their learning through traditional means. Getting students to write questions may actually be more valuable than getting them to answer them, especially in terms of providing evidence of understanding.

While these ideas work well to identify sticking points, students writing and/or asking questions offers real opportunities to stretch reasoning and to demonstrate evidence of higher order thinking.   For example, asking students to come up with questions that require inference or prediction offers visible evidence of their ability to think at these levels, arguably in ways that are more challenging than simply requiring responses to teacher-generated questions.

Students Write Questions

For example:

- About what they would like to know on a new topic
- To ask the teacher or other students in order to assess their learning
- To demonstrate their learning, misconceptions, areas they would like to explore.

The classroom could have a box there students can deop questions at the end of a lesson.

Or a plenary could involve students writing questions that the class then work on together, or which forms the basis of the next lesson.

(c) Mike Gershon

I was recently teaching an observed lesson with a group of 12 and 13 year old students in South Australia - my brief was to model inclusive classroom strategies as the basis for later discussions with the teachers - and I was picking up a lesson on inference.   My initial plenary activity made it clear that, while the students had a grasp of the concept of inference, and could answer inferential questions, they could not articulate what it actually meant to infer. However, once the class was challenged to come up with questions that required inferential thinking, their understanding and application of the process grew in leaps and bounds.

A helpful teaching point is to demonstrate how, while answers requiring knowledge and understanding can be highlighted in the text, actually cutting out the line of text and pasting it in as an answer also makes the point - this cannot work for inference. Concrete examples set the ball rolling: "What questions might you ask to find out if someone understood why the character was feeling sad, happy, etc.?"

Challenging the class to ask and answer inferential questions in this way quickly makes the point that, while the answers are often obvious, they cannot be found 'on the page' or 'on the lines'; the answers to inferential questions are always off the lines and even beyond the lines. Cross-referencing with examples from TV programmes – Sherlock Holmes, CSI, etc. – also helps to drive the point home.

It was particularly rewarding to observe the way the priority learners rose to this challenge, demonstrating a real grasp of inferential questioning in ways that were unlikely to shine through had they been working on a traditional comprehension activity. Students somewhere on the Autism Spectrum valued the step by step processing of identifying clues and drawing conclusions and students on the Dyslexia Spectrum enjoyed opportunities to think outside of the lines to pull in extraneous detail. Also, those who typically struggled to maintain their focus were fascinated by the opportunity to challenge the thinking of their peers in a real life situation.

The next step is asking students to evaluate the answers of their peers in relation to these questions, which takes the activity up to another level entirely. Providing question stems from Bloom's Taxonomy can offer a concrete and explicit starting point.

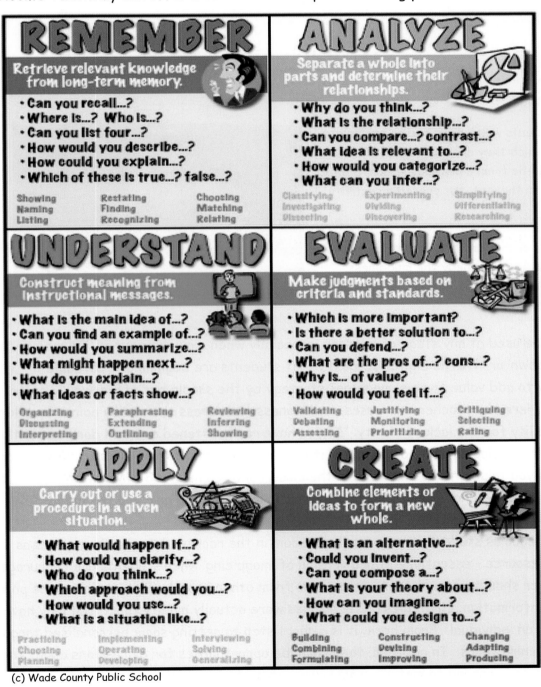

(c) Wade County Public School

An effective challenge is to allocate a points value to each domain as follows:

Remembering questions - 1 point   Analysing questions – 4 points
Understanding questions – 2 points   Evaluating questions – 5 points
Applying questions – 3 points   Creating questions – 6 points

Then challenge pairs, groups or tables to earn 20 points by creating as few questions as possible on the topic in hand. This can be achieved by writing three 'Creating' questions and one 'Understanding' or any other possible combination.

Another very useful strategy, again from the work of Mike Gershon, is 'Muddiest Point'.

Muddiest Point

Students write down one or two points on which they are least clear. This could be from a previous lesson, a topic within the unit, the preceding activity, etc.

The teacher and the class then work together to remedy the muddiness.

(c) Mike Gershon

This can be used at any stage of a lesson, especially when a quick round of 'Thumbs up/Thumbs down' or 'Traffic Lights' suggests that students are beginning to struggle.
It is easy to add value to this important strategy by the simple but effective 'C3B4Me' process. Here the teacher expresses a willingness to address the muddy points by taking responsibility for any lack of clarity: "If you have really listened and still don't get it then it is my fault. Apologies, I need to explain it better". But then comes the spin: "But before I do I want you to see if the answer is in the classroom, you must 'C3B4Me', that is, "ask three people to help you and if they can't, then come to me and I will give you the answer".

C3B4Me requires students to access the wisdom in the room and to use their peers as a learning resource – essentially, it is a version of 'magpieing' when students are encouraged to look over shoulders and 'steal' useful ideas from other people. This can make the point that the information, strategies or techniques were actually made explicit but may have been missed by an individual. From here, it is a short step to setting some personalised targets for maintaining focus. In addition, there may be opportunities for discussions about the need to develop and respond to metacognitive awareness of when focus is being lost.

There are also obvious 'students write questions' opportunities stemming from this activity. These activities are designed to produce visible evidence of learning and, regardless of outcomes, should determine the next stage. AfL will validate the lesson planning for some students as it confirms the positive impact on their learning. For others it may indicate the need for some personalisation in order to consolidate or re-visit important techniques or concepts.

> **A word to the wise:** C3B4Me and Magpieing presuppose a responsible approach from individuals as they move around the class. This is best presented as a privilege that will be lost if not used appropriately. Also consider identifying students who will wear the 'mantle of the expert' and be first port of call for certain queries. This offers a great opportunity to tap into the specialist expertise of some of the priority learners and, in appropriate circumstances, consider taking certain experts out of the process to encourage others to engage - "You can't ask Paul or Rashid at this time".

3. 'Feed forward' feedback that enables learners to identify their next steps

In a message to new teachers, Phil Beadle[6] writes:

> *"Make no mistake: this is the most important thing you do as a teacher. All the other stuff is of no use whatsoever if you don't mark your books properly".*

His article, which is a very good read, makes a strong case for the need for thorough marking and few would disagree. However, if priority learners are to demonstrate progress over time, Total Teaching requires a more personalised marking process, if only because vulnerable students may struggle to read typical marking comments. Also, some marking protocols can be extremely difficult to follow, with so many different symbols for different errors that it requires a degree in cryptography to interpret them.

Leaving aside levels and grades, marking is, above all else, about dialogue between student and teacher – the teacher asks questions in the form of a task, the student responds to the question in the form of an assignment. Then the teacher responds to the answers in the form of marking and, hopefully, the student responds by modifying the next piece of work.

What distinguishes a Total Teacher is the quality, nature and purpose of the marking, the marking of most teachers gives feedback, telling students how they have done – marking done by Total Teachers feeds forward, telling students how they can make it better next time.

Here is an important paradigm shift because it challenges students to improve next time, without going through a laborious and demoralizing process of unpacking all the errors in the previous piece. Many priority learners already lack confidence in their academic abilities and associate corrections with failure, regardless of the colour of pen, highlighter or whatever other approach is currently in place to obscure the fact that errors have been made. This explains why they find drafting so difficult and unrewarding. A drafted piece, full of deletions and substitutions, looks ugly and smacks of failure. On the other hand, priority learners must come to view errors as building blocks to future achievement, the key question being, "How do we get them to this position?"

Step 1 – Mark less to get more

This is about personalized target marking which, for some students, could mean only marking anything which is right – maybe the only thing that is right – in a piece of work. The purpose is to undo the damage caused by 'one size fits all' marking, which is usually driven by a school's marking policy. Here we have a problem – policy is policy and it is there to be followed.

On the other hand, all schools make accommodations for students which 'bend' policy so there is a mandate for seeking permission to accommodate the needs of certain students by marking differently for a while. The phrase 'for a while' is key, we are not talking about a long-term change in the way things are done, merely an accommodation for a period in order to help certain students move onwards and upwards. It is also important to celebrate having the confidence to go for it by ignoring the error and focusing on what is almost within reach. I have had this conversation many times and have usually carried the day – the key seems to be to use the phrase "Let's do this for a while until confidence grows".

> **A word to the wise**: This accommodation in marking needs to be discussed with parents/carers as well as with team leaders/line managers. Even 'helicopter parents' can be helped to understand the need for target marking by pointing out that highlighting 'fotosynthesis' as an error does not help when their child is struggling to spell 'cat' – far better to celebrate getting close enough to this complex jargon word.

Step 2 – Marking for metacognition

This is about responsibility – basically by addressing the question, "Who does the work belong to and who is responsible for the quality". The problem with 'death by deep marking', apart from insulting students by defacing their work, is the messaging, which is that the teacher will take responsibility for identifying all the issues. Marking for metacognition challenges students to recognize their typical errors and take responsibility, initially for finding them and, later, for correcting them. Ultimately, the aim is to develop the inhibitory controls to avoid making them in the first place, but to stop spelling 'any' with an 'e' may require changing the habits of a lifetime.

A good place to start is 'dots in the margin'. These can mean negotiating with a student to create a personalized marking plan. At one level, the dot can mean, "Find one spelling mistake on this line and highlight it". Realistically there may be more than one error on a line but asking the student to identify one is a fair challenge. Note the task here is to identify, not to correct – corrections can come later.

At another level, the dot can mean, "Find and correct one word" – but this must be done without a dictionary because dictionaries, with the possible exception of David Mosely's 'ACE Dictionary', only work for people whose phonics are secure and can therefore spell. My advice is to keep dictionaries right out of the process at all times and to rely on the process of 'serial probability' (the odds that the letters appear in certain combinations) to make the appropriate correction. Careful selection of target words can link the correction process to the current stage of a phonic programme or to a previously taught spelling pattern.

This also creates good opportunities for peer work where a partner gives the student the correct letters to make the target word and guides the 'make and break' process. Of course, in the real world most people use Google or Wikipedia to check spellings so it is important to build in the opportunity to go on line as part of the spelling process.

Step 3 – Where are you now?
I have already cast doubt on the value of copying objectives or learning goals from the board. However organising activities that enable students to engage with the goals is a very good thing indeed, especially for priority learners. Asking students to read the goals and then 'Articulate then Answer' (Mike Gershon) works well to set the ball rolling.

Articulate then Answer

Give students the opportunity to articulate their thinking before answering:

- 30 seconds silent thinking before giving any answers
- Brainstorm in pairs first for 2-3 minutes, order your ideas
- Write down some thoughts before answering
- Discuss your ideas with your neighbour first then answer

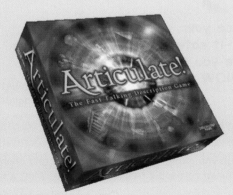

(c) Mike Gershon

Then a simple 5 point scale or the 'smiley faces' below allow students to indicate where they think are they with regard to achieving the outcome. Total Teachers will pay particular attention to the responses of more vulnerable individuals during this process in order to ensure that the planned lesson has appropriate starting points for the range of abilities, needs, competencies and skills in the class.

As ever, this requires an investment of time if it is to be effective. This is where a wise teacher has already printed the outcomes on strips of paper, possibly along with the title and date, to allow slower writers to stick them into their books and use the 'copying time' to establish where they are now and what they need to do next. Copying goals from the board does not seem to work for many students – but asking "Where are you in relation to the goals and what might you have to do to get there?" definitely does.

Step 4 – Next steps?

This 'Next Steps Indicator' is a combination of a Bloom Taxonomy triangle combined with a hierarchy of questions relating to pollution. Asking students to identify where they think they are now carries the implied challenge of being able to prove it – so the next task is to "Show you know – in any way you feel to be appropriate". The beauty of this approach is that it empowers quick thinking students with weak basics to demonstrate their understanding in preferential ways as well as giving teachers a quick overview of the current impact and effectiveness of teaching and learning.

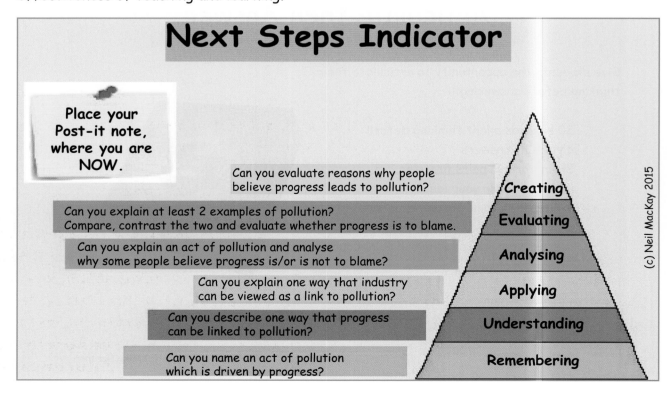

4. Empowering students to be in charge of their own learning

There is always a buzz in a lesson in which students are in charge of their own learning. The process needs a brave teacher who is prepared to go with the flow of learning rather than try to impose too much pedagogy – after all, it is the students who are supposed to be doing the work! The teacher needs to be brave because it is often hard to predict the actual outcomes when students are in the flow.

While it is usually possible to guarantee that learning will be taking place, it may be harder to actually quantify what is being learnt at any given point. Vulnerable students, often with clearly defined learning needs, can flourish when empowered to show what they know in preferential ways and the chunking approach that is implicit with assessment for learning. This implies that they have sufficient metacognitive knowledge of how best to tackle certain tasks and a willingness to be guided towards these 'best ways'. Also implicit is a willingness to take risks and to cope with getting it wrong without gratuitous displays of unnecessary emotion. I say 'gratuitous' because many students have learnt how to manipulate their teachers, support workers and parents by over-reacting to mistakes to such an extent that adults can be reluctant to push them to the next level of competence.

In effect this means that these students are rarely working in their Zone of Proximal Development with correspondingly weak gains in strategies, skills, techniques and competencies – they are effectively stuck through their overly emotional response to failure. The mantra 'No failure, only feedback' helps to emphasize the importance of errors as a natural consequence of the learning process. Re-framing failure as part of the process takes patience, skill and, on occasion, a degree of counselling for students and parents/carers.

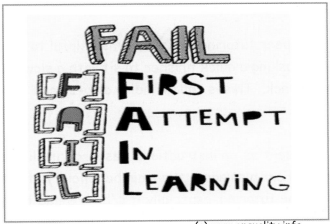

(c) www.onquality.info

However, it is important that the consequences of mistakes or failure are proportionate and personalised. Students on the Autism Spectrum can find mistakes incredibly threatening but, with patience, can appreciate that addressing errors helps them achieve their goal of a good piece of work. Discussing ways to identify errors can be helpful. Some of my students prefer comments, etc. on post-it notes so they can respond in their own way without having their work 'disfigured' by my corrections.

Those on the Dyslexia Spectrum often have well-developed emotional responses to failure which are often little more than avoidance strategies. Once it is accepted that the long-term impact of such responses will be to render individuals unemployable, it is possible to engage in meaningful discussions about using mistakes to move forward. Moving forward is the key.

A word to the wise: Please do not ask vulnerable students to do best copies – this is a total waste of time. However, a better version with different mistakes is always of value.

An unwanted side effect of providing support for vulnerable students is the risk of 'learned helplessness'. This occurs when a student learns that finding something hard means that someone will do it for them. There is a fine balance between empowering, pushing too hard or too soon for independence and wrapping up in cotton wool. I have certainly done all three as I strive to find ways to move vulnerable students forward. The hardest students to move forward are those who have learnt to manipulate their support as described above.

Setting individual goals linked to personalised marking works well, as does setting them up to succeed during the early stages by creating an 'error free' learning environment. By this I mean setting tasks which are really too easy and which guarantee success. Once confidence has been established it is easy to gently increase the degree of difficulty, especially when accompanied by 'expectation setting' comments like, "You are going to find some of this a challenge – 5/8 will be a great score," especially when the task has been chosen to ensure a score of at least 6! There is always a place for creative 'kidology' in Total Teaching!

5. Harnessing the power of peer tutoring – students as 'instructional resources' for each other

To understand what effective peer tutoring looks like it is helpful to start with the negative, peer tutoring is definitely not asking a quick finisher to sit with a slow finisher to 'help' or, even worse, to keep them on track. This is child minding at best and, at worst, risks upsetting both parties.

On the other hand, using a student as 'an instructional resource' implies a degree of forethought and preparation. For this reason the main beneficiary of effective peer tutoring is the student actually doing the tutoring, especially if s/he has had time to prepare. A typical scenario could be:

- A student is struggling with an aspect of work – the aspect is within the ZPD and is almost within reach.

- Instead of offering help at this point, the teacher challenges the student to prepare the aspect to teach to the group – this makes a powerful homework task and is my preferred strategy

- If appropriate, the challenge can include creating an animated power point, a model or maybe a diagram with removable labels – basically anything to make the presentation as interactive and multi-sensory as possible.

- During the following lesson the student presents the aspect to the group as the peer tutor – effectively wearing the mantle of the expert.

Almost without exception, the peer tutor has mastered the aspect and is ready to move on. The rest of the group also benefit from engaging with a presentation made in 'student speak' but there is little doubt who is the main beneficiary of the peer tutoring process.

Indeed research by the Sutton Trust, supported by John Hattie and Dylan Wiliam, suggests that effective peer tutoring can offer gains of 18 months in a year. This approach works really well for students on grade boundaries of high stakes testing protocols. The temptation is to mentor them – effectively to 'teach them harder'. Peer tutoring offers a much more effective alternative.

References:

1. **Dylan Wiliam, Assessment for Learning: Why, What, and How?**
   Institute of Education, Univ. of London 2006

2. **Sutton Trust, Education Endowment Foundation**
   Downloads from: http://educationendowmentfoundation.org.uk/toolkit/toolkit-a-z/

3. **John Hattie & Helen Timperley, The Power of Feedback**
   IN Review of Educational Research, March 2007 Vol. 77, No.1

4. **Dylan Wiliam & Paul Black, Inside the Black Box**
   Raising standards through classroom assessment
   GL Assessment 1990

5. **Mike Gershon, Assessment for Learning Toolkit**
   Download from: http://mikegershon.com/resources

6. **Phil Beadle, How to Teach**
   Crown House Publishing   June 2010

Chapter 6

Total Teaching
for Self-Directed Learning

A core principle of Total Teaching is accepting the preference paradigm, that Dyslexia, ASD and ADHD are best seen as preferred ways of learning. It follows, therefore, that these preferences can be expressed through choices and decisions through the seven stages of Self-directed learning (SDL).

1.   Interest
2.   Confidence
3.   Knowledge of personal learning needs
4.   Time management skills and support
5.   Self-evaluation of progress
6.   Easy access to resources
7.   Motivation

1. Interest

The process begins with the creation of a series of personalised, high interest activities as the basis for decision making. This can be personalised for different preferences:

- Students on the Dyslexia Spectrum may appreciate being presented with a range of choices to begin with and may well ignore them all to pursue a different direction

- Students on the Autism or ADHD Spectrum can be intimidated by too much choice and may appreciate a maximum of maybe two or three options. Forced choice can work well here. This is where one of the choices is overwhelmingly attractive in comparison to the others

The key seems to be to work from student interest to develop the skills and then apply the techniques to curriculum driven aspects. There is a clear mandate for this in many countries. My reading of national curriculum guidance in the UK, Australia, New Zealand and Hong Kong indicates an expectation that skills will be developed in a range of contexts before being applied to more exam driven situations.

The ideal climate to develop interest can be summed up as 'high challenge – low stress' which is easiest to engineer through activities that have a low entry level in terms of reading difficulty, etc. but high exit levels through a range of alternative evidence driven by higher order thinking skills. Giving students the freedom to choose badly and then insulating them from too many consequences will ultimately enable them to exceed their expectations, that is definitely the result of Total Teaching.

2. Confidence

The concept of order is variable – an orderly classroom for one teacher may be chaotic for another. I have already touched on the importance of including opportunities for 'safe mistakes' into the learning process for vulnerable students. The next step is to build in the expectation of a level of 'struggle', especially during the initialising and implementation phases of learning new skills and concepts. It is almost impossible for an individual to take their learning forward without going into their ZPD which can be a scary place for some. However, once students understand that 'implementation dip' is a necessary part of the process, they come to expect it and learn to deal with it.

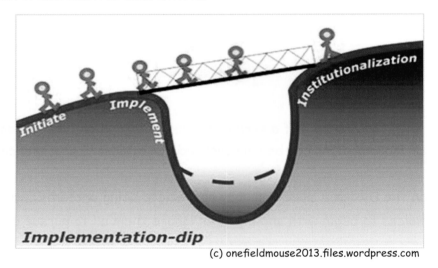

Implementation-dip

(c) onefieldmouse2013.files.wordpress.com

The graphic above shows how, in the early stages of expectation setting, careful scaffolding and the teaching of generic skills can lead students over the implementation dip. Generic skills include skimming and scanning, reading the first sentence of paragraphs to get the big picture, key word planning using mind-maps, flow-charts, etc. and the ability to 'talk' a plan as the precursor to writing.

However it is important not to insulate students totally from the consequences of certain decisions and actions. Developing confidence through obviously achievable tasks that are gradually levelled up to increasing levels of challenge builds habits for the future. A tangible sign that the process is working will be when, having been warned that the next task is going to be tricky and they will definitely struggle to achieve a target, the students' response is something like, "You were right – that was tough; what are we doing next?"

3. Knowledge of personal learning needs

Those questions "Where am I now?" and "What do I need to do to move on?" are part of the metacognitive process of developing self-knowledge. Christine Johnston[1] in her Learning Combinations Inventory offers insights into preferred ways of learning which lead naturally to personalisation strategies. The insights can be profound and often show why certain individuals are struggling in school. Their problems are often due to a mismatch between their preferred ways of learning and the ways they are actually being taught.

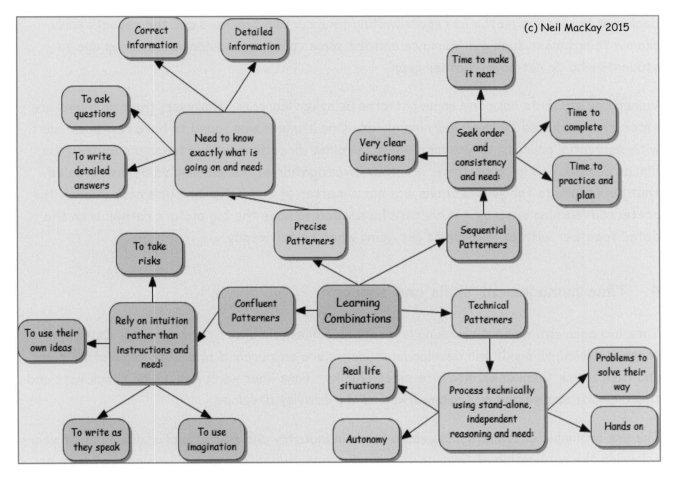

Many students need to know exactly what is going on before they start and cannot wait for an appropriate time to ask questions – as far as they are concerned, the appropriate time is now! They will score highly as precise patterners, possibly being somewhere on the Autism Spectrum.

Other students are incapable of hurrying – they take their time regardless of the situation because of their need for order and consistency. For them hitting a deadline is secondary to getting it much more 'perfect' than is necessary and their needs may also be associated with Autism at some level. We also have students who have little patience with anything that is not 'real' – they have no time for fiction or the arts, preferring to immerse themselves in real world situations and problems. Students on the ADHD Spectrum often operate effectively in clear cut, unambiguous real life situations because it cuts down options and avoids overstimulation.

Finally, there are students who very quickly form their own picture of how something could be done and are desperate to get going long before many teachers have finished giving instructions. Dyslexia may be the explanation here as they apply intuition and imagination to their tasks.

The important point to take from all of this is to appreciate how our staff rooms are full of colleagues who fit the above descriptions in various ways. School leaders soon come to realise, for example, that some colleagues are incapable of hitting deadlines because of their preoccupation with accuracy at the expense of efficiency. So effective leaders find ways to deal with the issues; maybe at report writing time certain teachers get the reports early. Simple things make such a difference and the same courtesy and consideration is due to students who do not have 'another gear'.

Vulnerable students have the same patterns as other learners. However, their patterns are often overshadowed by their learning needs. One student was found to have real problems with sequential processing, yet his failure to follow directions led his teachers to describe him as defiant, and uncooperative. Further investigation of his learning patterns revealed that his failure to follow directions was not a matter of bad behavior but a reflection of his preferred learning process – in his case he needed to have the big picture rather than the detail together with permission to get going when he felt ready.

4. Time management skills and support

Time management is about chunking and setting achievable short-term targets. Initially teacher driven, this skill will develop as students are encouraged to create 'big picture plans' and then break them down into bite-sized chunks. Time lines work well, as do check lists and these can be scaffolded or frameworked as the activity develops.

The use of simple checklists has been a focus in industry and education for a number of years following the publication of Gwande's[2] book. Letting students in on the sequence of lessons and assessments ahead of time is a version of the visible timetable on the wall which is often such a comfort to students.

Students on the Autism Spectrum appreciate knowing exactly what will happen next on a daily or lesson by lesson basis. While those on the ADHD Spectrum know that, if they can just hold it together for a few more minutes relief, in the form of a change of activity, is imminent. Regardless of learning preference and learning need, all students benefit from knowing the big picture and having the opportunity to receive as much detail as they need before engaging with a task. The skill of the Total Teacher lies in judging when to let students loose. It is also important for students to appreciate that, in the real world, doing what they are asked to do, in the way it is required and within a set deadline, is a basic requirement of most jobs. So we do them no favours if we do not set them up with the skills and mindset necessary to perform in a working environment where the ethos is 'My way or the highway'!

5. Self-evaluation of progress

Self-directed learning requires students to own the process and to make decisions about what they are doing, how effective they are and what to do next. Therefore, it is equally important that they own the process of evaluation. Checklists can be helpful to ensure that all required elements are present and provide a powerful, supportive scaffold for vulnerable students, enabling them to identify for themselves any gaps in their work and their next steps. Self evaluation also seems to work best when students own the success criteria, maybe working in pairs to decide what the finished piece should include. Exemplar work from another group can be especially effective in this context.

Peer review against agreed criteria is also extremely effective - especially in the form of '2 stars and a wish'. It would be a mistake to assume that this technique is only for younger children. I used it as part of a report writing course for post graduate civil engineers who told me that reviewing the work of colleagues to seek out 'stars and wishes' was the most valuable part of the day.

6. Easy access to resources

Students who think quickly but have weak basic skills need carefully selected resources to enable them to engage quickly and effectively with a topic. But it is important to think beyond traditional print media, whether in books or online. Making sure that students have a list of key 'search words' will be helpful, as is limiting research to a few pre-selected websites. Any electronic media can be read aloud using existing software on most laptops, androids and IPads and there are a number of apps. The British Dyslexia Association features 'Natural Reader' on their website.

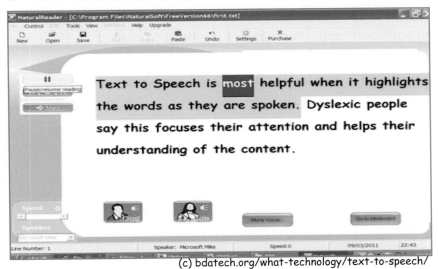

(c) bdatech.org/what-technology/text-to-speech/

There are a number of open source document summary programs. I suggest you have a look at **www.freesummarizer.com** which reduces documents to manageable proportions. Once a document is summarised, the use of a text to speech program becomes much more efficient and manageable.

7. Motivation

Many teachers appear to be frustrated by a perceived reluctance of vulnerable students to engage with lessons, often complaining that their students lack motivation. The 'chicken or egg' question is, quite simply, which comes first, motivation, success, or achievement? Successful teaching of vulnerable students relies on the ability to interest and engage students who, after years of struggling to achieve, are seriously questioning the value of being engaged.

Consequently, they can present as lacking in motivation. At one level this is probably true – they are definitely lacking in the motivation to enter into another spiral of institutionalised failure. On the other hand, if motivation actually does stem from success, the answer is clear – high interest, learning opportunities, personalised to minimise the chance of failure during the initial stages. As Dr Dylan Wiliam[3] observes:

> "When we start thinking about motivation as being an outcome rather than a cause of student achievement, we actually look at our classrooms in very different ways."

Although the focus is on vulnerable students, specifically those who may not learn easily when taught through traditional means, the strategies above have been identified as forming a core of best practice in any classsroom. The report, 'Exploring Effective Pedagogy in Primary Schools'[4] draws on dozens of research papers including 'EPPS in English and Maths', which contains observations from 125 different Year 5 classrooms. It concluded that teachers in excellent schools excel at:

- Ensuring that Assessment for Learning was part of lessons
- Providing sufficient opportunities for children to reflect on their learning

This proves, once again, that getting it right for vulnerable learners gets it right for all.

Recap

Issue 4 for Total Teaching is:

How do I keep track of quick thinking, slow delivering students in a busy classroom?

The Total Teaching solution is:

Splitting lessons into more bite sized chunks and monitoring impact through a range of assessment for learning techniques.

by

- Use chunking and stage reviews to get feedback about learning
- Notice and adjust – use feedback to fine tune the lesson as it develops
- Use the Assessment for Learning Toolkit
- Mark for success - use feed forward feedback wherever possible
- Consistently demonstrate that there is no failure only feedback
- Develop self-directed learners
- Hold on to the belief that motivation comes from success

References

1. **Christine Johnson, Using the Learning Combination Inventory**
   IN Educational Leadership, 1997 Vol. 55 No. 4

2. **Atul Gwande, The Checklist Manifesto: how to get things right**
   Profile Books   Jan 2011

3. **Dylan Wiliam, Excerpt from talk at Assessment Network Conference**
   University of Cambridge, 2006

4. **Iram Siraj-Blatchford, et al.**
   Exploring Effective Pedagogy in Primary Schools: Evidence from Research
   Download from: https://research.pearson.com/articles/explore-eppse.html

Chapter 7

Confidence and Risk Taking

Issue 5: My students lack confidence in their ability and will not take risks or stretch themselves.

Total Teaching and the Growth Mindset

To label or not to label – that is the question. Early intervention is recognised as being fundamental to a child's chances of overcoming perceived learning difficulties. But the very act of identification may come at a high cost, one which has the potential to limit future achievement and possibly even to damage the mental health of the adult to come. It seems that the very process of labelling a child as 'struggling'[1] has the potential to become far more than a self-fulfilling prophecy – it can actually change the way children perceive themselves, their place in the world and their potential for the future.

According to the work of Carol Dweck[2] and others, being labelled as 'bright' can be just as damaging. When teachers praise students for being smart it seems to have a negative impact on their performance; what Dweck refers to as the "inverse power of praise".   The work of Wulf Uwe Meyer[3], et al. launched this debate in 1979, where the researchers found that, by age 12, students believe praise from a teacher to be a sign of a lack of ability and the need for encouragement rather than a positive sign of success.

Experienced teachers of vulnerable learners appreciate how readily children associate praise with the negative rather than the positive; praising a learner for being 'good' almost invariably causes suspicion. It is almost possible to hear the thinking "Oh oh – what is s/he going to ask me to do now?"

The graphic overleaf summarises some of Dweck's findings. To identify the 'over-praised kid' try listening for 'inflected speech' where statements have the inflection of questions as the learner desperately seeks confirmation before committing fully to an opinion or answer. Often this is accompanied by constant eye checking to gauge a teacher's response.
In other words, the learner is following a low risk strategy of answering to please rather than expressing a view, committing to an answer or going for broke.

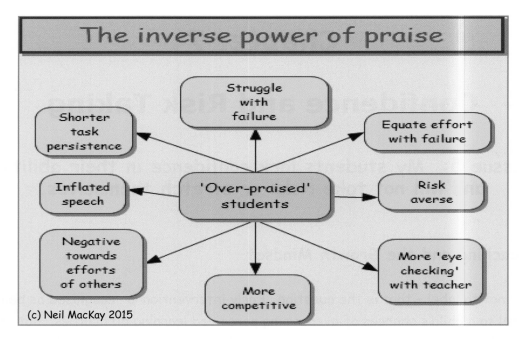

The inverse power of praise

Struggle with failure · Shorter task persistence · Equate effort with failure · Inflated speech · 'Over-praised' students · Risk averse · Negative towards efforts of others · More competitive · More 'eye checking' with teacher

(c) Neil MacKay 2015

The quality of questioning plays a large part in this process. Where teacher questioning is summative, designed to check memory and 'who is listening' (effectively operating at the lower levels of Bloom's Taxonomy) the consequences of being wrong can be serious. Where questioning is open and about creating, evaluating and analysing, the final outcome is only part of an important formative process.

I listened to a student using higher order thinking skills to explain how flying squirrels might have evolved into bats. He used a combination of evaluation and analysis to create a theory based around how DNA from moths eaten by the squirrels helped them to grow wings. While he was completely wrong in his final conclusion, he did some very powerful thinking along the way. The teacher celebrated the process of the student's thinking and used his theory to lead the class into genetics at a higher level. However had it been a high stakes 'right or wrong' question, it would have been impossible to acknowledge anything but a correct answer. Praising what is effectively an unearned 'gift' (being talented, gifted etc.) may actually do damage as students who, having learned that talent creates success without effort, have no strategies to use in situations where being talented is no substitute for hard work. Children who are constantly praised for 'trying hard' when they have not made any progress run a corresponding risk of learning that hard work cannot mitigate against failure, in both scenarios the language of the adult defines the resilience of the learner.

If the only acceptable outcome is a successful result, 'over-praised kids' at all levels of apparent ability, seem reluctant to take risks, especially when the risk involves extra effort. The equation is simple – if learners are judged on outcome alone, effort may not guarantee success so it may be better not to try. So learners with a history of success only attempt what they know they can do well and are reluctant to push themselves. Learners with a history of failure quickly appreciate that no amount of effort yields a desired result and so they either do not try or, as every teacher has experienced, they grossly over react to failure in unhelpful ways.

The message for the classroom

This research validates the approaches where the adult uses task specific praise to acknowledge tangible achievements that are under the control of the learner. Fortunately the solution seems to be reasonably straightforward – we need to praise the tangible – the hard work, energy, enthusiasm or the 'grit' that went into completing a task rather than praising 'smarts'.

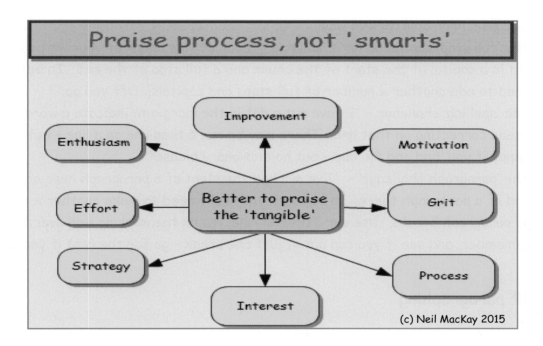

Dweck compared the results of two groups of students who were randomly praised either for being intelligent or for their efforts in solving puzzles. The group praised for their efforts improved their scores by more than 30% over a series of tests whereas the group praised for their intelligence scored 20% lower on the final activity. In her attempts to rationalise the findings, Dweck concludes that emphasising effort gives learners a variable they can control – more means better. There are interesting parallels with the world of sport where athletes are challenged to improve by small increments during a match or over a period of time. Emphasising natural intelligence or ability removes control from the learner – if they fail it must be because they do not have enough intelligence and there is nowhere to go for more – or so it seems.

Working SMART

The message for Total Teaching is clear – praise needs to be based upon something real and tangible, something that can be identified, targeted and developed. Teachers who set SMART targets (Specific, Measureable, Attainable, Realistic, Time-based) are already noticing differences in achievement and attainment as their students learn to associate increased effort with increased success in specific areas.

While some schools do this on a formal basis, task related targets and praise work especially well on a 'over the shoulder' marking basis as the teacher identifies a developmental aspect of an individual's work and sets a 'do-able' challenge.

Using SMART targets challenges for 'tangible praise' opportunities:

1. The 'wow word' challenge – "Can you use a powerful adjective in the next sentence?"
2. The 'starting with a conjunction' challenge – "I bet you can't begin a sentence with 'Because' in an appropriate way!"
3. The 'full stop/capital letter' challenge – "Look at this chunk of your writing. I have put in a capital at the start of the chunk and a full stop at the end. In between you need to add another x number of full stops and capitals. Off you go."
4. The 'spelling' challenge – "I have put a dot in the margin to indicate a word that needs correcting on that line. There may be more than one on a line – but I'll be happy if you 'find and fix' one – but no dictionary please!"
5. The 'paragraph challenge' - "I've marked the start of a paragraph here and the end of a paragraph there. In between you really need to make another x number of paragraph breaks. Use our TIP-TAP rule, it's on the working wall over there remember, and see if you can put in just one break – go for the rest if you can."

TIP –TAP paragraphing

You start a new paragraph when you change or bring in:

1. Time	"The volcano stopped erupting after a week and…"
2. Idea	"It is important that chickens have a fox proof run because"
3. Person	"When the donkey appeared, Shrek was not happy"
4. Theme/Topic	"On the other hand…"
5. Advert	Imagine you are writing a Soap for TV where could you put an advert break?
6. Picture	When does the picture in your head change?

Each of the challenges above offers opportunities for tangible praise, especially if the final instruction is to "Let me know when you have done/found 1, 2, whatever". This informal feedback loop builds in the opportunity to offer tangible praise, to re-set a target if it proves to be unattainable at this time or to offer a fresh challenge if appropriate.

Appropriate challenges are those which are just beyond the comfort zone of the students, effectively within their zone of proximal development (ZPD), where success is possible, but only with assistance or guidance.

Carol Dweck talks about the 'exuberance of learning' that a young child displays while acquiring the skills of walking and talking. For many, this exuberance continues during nursery/kindergarten as the way they are taught – hands on, plenty of repetition, small steps, discovery learning, low stress – mirrors the way they learn best.

During this period some children are already being recognised as solution focussed individuals who bring a unique view to solving problems in the classroom. Then a strange change begins to occur, the child continues to learn some things easily and effortlessly, while other things become more of a struggle. It is at this point that unnoticed learning differences actually begin to become learning difficulties.

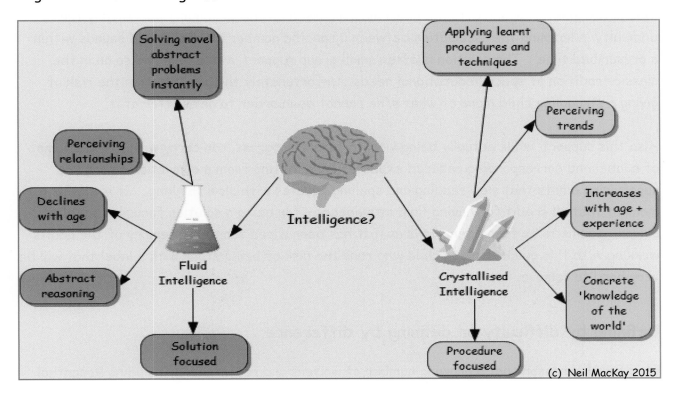

(c) Neil MacKay 2015

What is fascinating is that the difficulties tend to be with the acquisition of the skills and knowledge associated with crystalised intelligence, the intelligence that is based on remembering and applying rules and processes. This is the intelligence that is largely measured by high stakes testing where success, to a large extent, is little more than a function of recall.

The learning difficulties are initially often associated with learning rhymes, chants, clapping games, anything which requires remembering and repeating a sequence or process. To the experienced observer these difficulties are 'unexpected' in the light of clear aptitude in other areas. Unfortunately powerful fluid intelligence, strengths in abstract reasoning and problem solving, etc., while essential in the world of work and beyond, are not easy to measure. As a result they may not feature as much in high stakes testing; it is much easier to quantify, level and grade the ability to spell and read accurately, to answer questions/write at length in stylised ways and to apply taught and learnt processes and strategies to concrete situations.

The problems associated with learning clapping games, etc. quickly become compounded when it comes to learning to read and spell. Most schools have read and responded to the compelling evidence supporting the need for an awareness of phonemes, syllables and morphology. Most of the commonly used schemes are based around the initial requirement to learn a certain number of letter sounds each week. Here is where it becomes interesting – and sad, because our bright, problem solving, solution focussed child with fluid intelligence to burn suddenly hits a wall – an artificial wall – when required to learn another person's techniques, strategies and processes and apply them to situations that seem pretty irrelevant at that moment in time.

This is the point at which attention becomes focussed on the 'problem' – specifically the difficulty in learning the association between a specific number of letters and sounds within a prescribed time. The solution is often small group support, extra help and so on in the classic tradition of special educational needs. Unfortunately this may also run the risk of giving a struggling child more of what s/he cannot do in order to get better at it.

Also this support, while actually being vital to future progress, can carry with it the stigma of a label and corresponding reduced expectation, resulting from a conviction among the supervising adults that slow reading and spelling equates with slow thinking. It is at this moment that all credit for having fluid intelligence – for being a solution focussed problem solver - seems to be forgotten. It is as if it has been wiped from the memory of the adults working with this quick thinking child who runs the risk of being stuck with a label that will be very hard to remove.

Defining by difficulty or defining by difference

It is for this reason that a growing number of writers and researchers, including Rosenthal and Jacobsen[4] and Hattie[5] argue that it is better not to label because it changes outcomes. We are not talking here about the impact of a quasi-medical label such as ADHD but actually labelling students as 'bright' or 'struggling' and formalising this by placements in certain groups, sets, tables or classes. It is interesting to reflect on the findings of the Sutton Trust on the negative impact of ability grouping on the achievement of vulnerable students.

The Trust's research suggests that such a placement can result in some students actually going backwards over a year. If this is accepted, it is likely to be because quick thinking, slow reading/spelling/writing students are being taught as if they are global slow learners, along with reduced expectations and lessons of inappropriate pace. All too quickly students pick up on the language of the adults around them and stop seeing themselves as quick thinkers. Instead they begin to share the view of their teachers and parents that they are slow learners and somehow less worthy than their peers.

I would argue that it is far better to move to a belief that all students are capable of good progress despite different starting points and varied rates of progress. In fact, many so called 'vulnerable learners' may be making more progress that those recognised as being gifted and talented – often this group is stalled but, because of overall high attainment, the issues can be swept under the table.

Is it about 'brainwashing'?

Eric Jensen[6] goes as far as to suggest that we should be actively brainwashing our students to alter negative perceptions. He reports Hattie 's conclusion that one of the single greatest factors contributing to student achievement is the student's prediction about how they will do in school. Some students believe they are stuck at their present level and, as Jensen remarks, "This 'fixed mindset' is deadly".

In Hong Kong many students struggle with English as a second language in primary school and carry very negative attitudes to the subject into secondary school. Secondary teachers of English on my Thematic Courses at Hong Kong Polytechnic University regularly report that the students seem to hate English and, by association, hate the teachers as well as they anticipate another five years of failure and potential humiliation. This is a concrete example of the impact of students' negative predictions about how they will do. It is compounded by an over reliance on the teaching of grammatical patterns and exceptions rather than re-focussing the students on spoken language.

Following the courses, the teachers are working hard to break this cycle of failure and, by engineering early and sustained success, are beginning to effectively 'brainwash' students into positive perceptions of themselves as successful learners of English. I recommend watching Carol Dweck talking about the importance of positive metacognitive 'self-talk' on her YouTube channel.

In particular she asks what the voice in the head is saying and identifies the typically negative workings of the fixed mindset as it wears away at the learner by saying things like "Oh you'd better not make a mistake", or "You'd better look smart – we are judging you". Dweck contrasts this with the language of the growth mindset, the language of 'I can' which has an inner dialogue which says, "Here is an opportunity I can learn from. I feel smart when I do something different".

Total Teachers are aware of the vulnerabilities of students who, through persistent failure in response to inappropriate tasks, tests and expectations, have come to doubt their ability to achieve at anything, despite skills in all sorts of areas that might not be valued in school. This mirrors the anecdotal evidence from high achieving Dyslexic adults, many of whom report that they had to leave school to become successful.

Jensen uses Dweck's work to model some growth mindset statements which should become part of the 'language toolkit' of Total Teachers:

"You really studied for your English test, and your improvement shows it. You read the material over several times, outlined it, and tested yourself on it. That really worked!"

"I like the way you tried all kinds of strategies on that math problem until you finally got it."

"It was a long, hard assignment, but you stuck to it and got it done. You stayed at your desk, kept up your concentration, and kept working. That's great!"

"I like that you took on that challenging project for your science class. It will take a lot of work – doing the research, designing the machine, buying the parts, and building it. You're going to learn a lot of great things."

Recap

Issue 5 for Total Teaching is

My students lack confidence in their ability and will not take risks or stretch themselves

The Total Teaching strategy is

Using 'praise for improvement' to develop the growth mindset in our students

by:

- Praising tangibles rather than gifts
- Appreciating that the concept of growth mindset is supported by research – good science
- Learning how to grow abilities while accepting failures as tools for growth
- Listening out for that fixed mindset voice – when you hear it, talk back with a growth mindset voice. If you hear "I can't do it" add "Yet"

References

1. **John Hattie, Visible Learning**
   IN Educational Leadership, 1997 Vol. 55 No. 4

2. **Carol Dweck, The Growth Mindset**
   Profile Books   Jan 2011

3. **Wulf Uwe Meyer,   The informational value of evaluative behaviour: Influences of praise and blame on perceptions of ability**
   IN   Journal of Educational Psychology: Vol. 71(2)   April 1979

4. **Robert Rosenthal and Lenore Jacobson, Pygmalion in the classroom: Teacher Expectation and Pupils' Intellectual Development**
   Crown House Publishing, 2003

5. **John Hattie, Visible Learning for Teachers: Maximizing impact on learning**
   Routledge, 2011

6. **Eric Jensen, Should you be into brainwashing?**
   http://www.jensenlearning.com/news/brainwashing/brain-based-teaching

Chapter 8

Decoding and Phonics

Issue 6: My students have had years of phonics and still struggle to decode and encode despite abilities in other areas

Total Teaching and phonics

Few would argue that the core of learning to read and spell effectively is phonemic awareness, the automatic association of letters and sounds. Interestingly there seems to be a residual belief in some parts of the world, despite overwhelming evidence to the contrary, that all students will pick up reading and spelling by the 'osmosis method' known as whole word/whole language. Basically the view that enough exposure to print ensures the development of reading. While this does actually work for many students, for many others it has proved to be a disaster and serves, once more, to emphasise the importance of teaching the students rather than the programme, the method or the current doctrine.

The skills an experienced reader uses to cope with an unfamiliar word such as 'rhinotillexomania' (obsessive nose picking) will probably be a combination of whole word and phonic strategies, the balance being determined by individual preference. So it would seem logical to aim to equip emerging readers with both sets of skills in order, ultimately, to enable them to make metacognitive choices about their 'best ways'. The big question, of course, is where to start. The big answer is, of course, the explicit and systematic teaching of the sounds that make up the alphabetic code and the skills of blending/decoding for reading and segmenting/encoding for spelling.

While most practicing teachers are convinced of the need for phonemic and phonological awareness, discussions with young teachers in the southern hemisphere in particular suggest that not all university schools of education appear to get the message. Research supports starting with the cognitive skills of putting sounds together to synthesise words (encoding for reading) and breaking words down into their constituent sounds (decoding for spelling) in a hierarchical approach which starts with phonemic awareness into phonological processing and culminates, via fluency, in comprehension.

From here it is a short step to reading with metacognition as students are empowered to choose reading techniques appropriate for the task in hand, moving effortlessly from skimming/scanning to deep reading.

Steps to Reading Proficiency

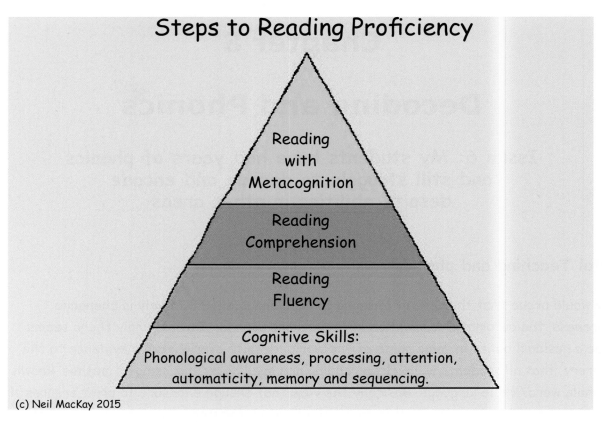

(c) Neil MacKay 2015

To be of any real value as a tool the process needs to be automatic, at a virtual stimulus response level - 'see it/hear it, do it'. The need to pause for thought or to remember and apply a taught strategy seems to cause the process to break down as students are forced to rely on their crystallised intelligence rather than the more spontaneous fluid reasoning. Rule based procedures work well for some students but not others, as ever, one size cannot fit all.

The importance of phonics as the cornerstone of reading and spelling can be likened to the use of stabiliser wheels when learning to ride a bike. For some the wheels give stability and security during a step-by-step learning process which develops into exploration and risk taking without consequence. Others need little more than a firm hand on the saddle, a good push and they are away.

Unfortunately there is a third group which, despite endless practice and opportunity, find riding with or without the stabilisers equally challenging and may never go on to become skilled riders. This group will go on to find alternative and equally satisfying means of transportation.

So the rule based, procedural drilling approach of many successful phonic programmes is exactly what some students need to tap into their crystallised intelligence. It suits their preference for the application of techniques that can be applied in most situations. Others seem to springboard almost effortlessly from phonemic awareness to whole word reading and spelling. This group will require careful differentiation and personalisation in order to develop their skills in ways that suit their learning preferences.

The third group require an eclectic approach, typically grounded on an evidence based phonic program but with the addition of a variety of materials in order to consolidate and reinforce skills and concepts. Some programmes may not provide enough opportunities for overlearning for some students and this is where the 'mastery rule' needs to be applied; if the students are not at an 80% success level they are not ready to move on.

The ability to add value to a valid, evidence based phonic programme is a key skill, requiring specialist training, expertise, confidence and careful monitoring for impact. This process of personalisation is particularly important for members of our third group, the individuals who find phonic approaches challenging because they struggle to 'hear' the sounds as they attempt to decode and encode. The Sutton Trust[1] adds support to the need to teach the student rather than the programme:

> "There is some evidence that particular approaches such as synthetic phonics may be more beneficial than analytic approaches, however the evidence here is less secure and it is probably more important to match the teaching to children's particular needs and systematically teach the sound patterns with which they are not yet confident."

Despite this difficulty, the Rose Report[2] observes that:

> "For most children, it is highly worthwhile and appropriate to begin a systematic programme of phonic work by the age of five, if not before for some children..."

and most practitioners would agree.

So phonemic awareness is a very desirable 'must have', ideally at a level of unconscious automaticity. I say "very desirable" in the certain knowledge that, for some extremely bright and talented individuals, this automaticity will be very hard come by, if at all, and we may need to find ways around and through the problem. Identifying students who are struggling to achieve automaticity can be done by screening. This is being done in the UK using a statutory non-word reading test[3] with all 5 year old students, described as follows:

> "The phonics screening check is a short, simple assessment to make sure that all pupils have learned phonic decoding to an appropriate standard by the age of 6. All year 1 pupils in maintained schools, academies and free schools must complete the check. The phonics check will help teachers identify the children who need extra help so they can receive the support they need to improve their reading skills. These children will then be able to retake the check in year 2. The check comprises a list of 40 words and non-words which the child will read one-to-one with a teacher".

The phonics test is designed to identify those students who are reading quite well using their sight vocabulary but who are not developing appropriate word attack skills, hence the use of non words like 'vap' and 'bim'. At the moment it is not norm-referenced and it would probably be a grave mistake to make it so. We really do not need another league table based on the performance of 5 year old students, because, in the current form, it provides a very pragmatic 'can they/can't they' assessment which readily informs the next step of teaching.

An alphabet arc as an informal phonic screener

Assessment for learning using an alphabet arc can also be effective and is easy to use.

(c) kidsonthegrow.blogspot.com

A student sits with an adult who points to random letters on the arc, asking, "What's that sound? What's this sound?"

Note. It is the sound that is being asked for, not the letter name – this is critical!

Very quickly the adult will get a feel for the student's level of phonemic awareness and can make an informed decision about next steps, maybe a more formal assessment, maybe some targeted intervention. It is important that the adult points to letters at random during both the assessment process and later as part of intervention.

Spotting 'unexpected difficulties' is the key here. If the student is having problems picking up sound–symbol correspondence in relation to age/ability appropriate speed of acquisition in other areas then the sticking point is unlikely to be lack of ability. We are probably looking at something more specific. What is essential is to guard against any view that slow reading goes hand in hand with slow thinking. For some reason hyperlexic students and those for whom English is a second or additional language, who may read accurately with little comprehension, can sometimes be perceived to be more able than students who read hesitantly but whose comprehension exceeds their ability to decode.

Peer Tutoring with an alphabet arc

Laminated copies of an alphabet arc provide opportunities for a range of peer driven activities, especially at the start of a day or after break/recess. It is easy to train students to play 'What's that sound?' with a partner and from here it is a short step to a range of blending activities. Partner 1 has a list of appropriate words, chooses a word and points to each letter in turn saying 'What's that sound?' Partner 2 says each sound and then is asked to blend them into the word. These can include c-v-c words and blends, building up to digraphs and schwa. Working memory can also be stretched by adding two syllable words or more – 'sausages' is a great challenge!

Measuring impact – using reading quotients

The concept of 'enough impact' is critical. For example, a student aged 10 with a reading age of 8 years is 2 years behind. After a year of support the reading age could be 9.00, which could mistakenly be seen as making progress. However, the student is also a year older so the 2-year gap remains – the programme has not had enough impact. To achieve meaningful impact a programme has to deliver, say, 14 months progress in a year, preferably more if the gap is to narrow.

An effective way to identify progress is to work in reading quotients rather than reading ages. The reading quotient can be determined by dividing a child's reading-age test scores by their chronological age and multiplying by 100.

Reading Quotient

$$\frac{\textbf{Reading age}}{\textbf{Chronological age}} \times \textbf{100}$$

So if we take a 10 year old student with a reading age of 8.00 years, that produces a reading quotient of 80. At the next test our student is now 11.00 and has a reading age of 9 years and 3 months (9.25 years). Dividing the new reading age of 9.25 years by chronological age gives a reading quotient of 83, so we can conclude that the programme is having a positive impact. This method also allows comparison between students with different birth dates. In the western hemisphere having an August birthday is often seen as a potential disadvantage as it means that a child will be one of the youngest in the class, with all the implied 'readiness' issues. Converting reading and spelling ages to quotients enables direct comparison between individuals regardless of age.

Where should support take place?

One-to-one tuition and small group tuition are effective interventions. However, the cost effectiveness of one-to-two and one-to-three indicates that greater use of these approaches would be productive in schools. Short, regular sessions (about 30 minutes, 3-5 times a week) over a set period of time (6-12 weeks) appear to result in optimum impact.

However there is no strong evidence that one-to-one is better than paired tuition or intensive small group teaching, and in some circumstances evidence suggests that pairs make better progress than individual pupils. Evidence also suggests tutoring should be additional or supplemental to normal instruction, rather than as a replacement and that teachers should monitor progress to ensure the tutoring is beneficial.

Recap

Issue 6 for Total Teaching is:

**My students have had years of phonics and still struggle
to decode and encode despite abilities in other areas**

The Total Teaching strategy is:

**To be aware of individual preferences and monitor
the impact of intervention to ensure enough impact**

by:

- Teaching phonemic and phonological awareness to mastery via synthetic phonics where possible. It will be the cornerstone of reading and spelling success for most students
- Being prepared to add value to well-respected phonic programmes. Few have the flexibility to meet the needs of all learners at all times
- Monitoring impact carefully. Consider using reading quotients
- Being aware of the needs of some students who are more effective when using approaches demanding more eclectic fluid intelligence strategies rather than rule based concrete intelligence approaches
- Using a non-word phonic screen. Use it for spelling as well as reading – and make sure the assessment turns into action
- Looking for opportunities to create small groups of 2:1 or even 3:1. Groupings of 1:1 may not automatically be best for all at all times

References:

1. **Sutton Trust, Education Endowment Foundation**
   Downloads from: http://educationendowmentfoundation.org.uk/toolkit/toolkit-a-z/

2. **Jim Rose,   Independent review of the teaching of early reading**
   Dept. of Children, Families and Schools March 2006   (para. 89)

3. **Dept. for Education, Phonics screening check**
   https://www.gov.uk/government/publications/phonics-screening-check-2014-materials

Chapter 9

Comprehension Activities

Issue 7: How do I include quick thinking, slow decoders in comprehension activities?

The focus here is on students who can understand complex information when it is presented orally or in the media but who struggle to decode at an age appropriate level. The passages are likely to be within a student's zone of proximal development (ZPD) in terms of knowledge, understanding and concept development, the barriers being decoding and/or fluency.

Many schools in many countries use versions of guided reading to teach specific reading skills and this approach seems to be universally accepted and respected. Typically, it involves a teacher working with small groups of students with similar levels of reading accuracy and fluency. Texts are chosen to present opportunities for problem solving but also to be read with a degree of fluency when supported by a teacher, teacher aide or other skilled adult. Successful schools interpret guided reading to suit the needs of their students and develop a house style. Burkins & Croft[1] suggest that a typical approach will include:

- Working with small groups
- Matching student reading ability to text levels
- Giving everyone in the group the same text
- Introducing the text
- Listening to individuals read
- Prompting students to integrate their reading processes
- Engaging students in conversations about the text

The Total Teacher will immediately spot the problem with guided reading, it limits choice of text to current levels of decoding and fluency, effectively condemning the target students to material of low interest with little 'stretch' in terms of higher level thinking. Also it can ignore a fundamental truth, which is that some quick thinkers will rarely manage to put these skills together into what Marie Clay calls a 'smooth integrated system'. For them, guided reading can be a source of frustration and sometimes condescension as they battle with passages that are of limited interest or cognitive challenge.

Paired reading

One solution is paired reading. This involves two students or a student and an adult reading a passage together as one voice. If one student ends up reading alone the process has gone wrong. It is essential to appreciate that paired reading is not "You read, then I read". Reading in unison gives the weaker decoder confidence because s/he knows that the lead reader will cue all the words, thus ensuring instant success and access. The stronger decoder also benefits by being challenged to "tell the story with the voice", which requires an understanding of the text.

Paired reading can operate at several levels in a classroom. Experience suggests it to be the very best way to improve fluency, comprehension and enjoyment of reading, although some students may find the process hard to accept at first. The power of paired reading lies in the opportunity to engage students with texts that stretch their reasoning and higher order thinking but which, under normal circumstances, would be beyond their current level of decoding.

If I was asked to improve the comprehension and fluency at a whole class or whole school level I would do it through paired reading. Typical pairings could include:

- Stronger decoder with weaker decoder
- Good decoder with poor comprehension with poor decoder with weak comprehension – this works well in EAL/ESL settings
- Students with similar levels of decoding to stretch comprehension

A pragmatic way to pair a class is as follows:

- List the class in terms of decoding skills, from high to low
- Split the list in half
- Pair the 'top' students on each list and so on down the lists
- Adjust pairings according to social/emotional factors as appropriate and remember that a group of three will not work – this is 'paired reading'

It is also valid to list the class in terms of listening comprehension, the ability to understand via receptive language. This is a very different skill to decoding and is likely to produce a very different list.

Another powerful approach is to pair across age groups. Older students with weak decoding are often prepared to read 'easy' books with younger students, thus gaining the practice they need without damaging their self esteem.

Paired reading is a skill and needs to be taught. Lead readers have a particular responsibility to make the process work and the following principles are easy to establish and work well in most settings:

- Lead reader points to the words as they are read
- S/he reads at a comfortable pace and does not stop if the partner fails to decode a word. This is critical to maintaining flow, which is such a fundamental part of effective comprehension
- If a word cannot be read or a mistake is made, the lead reader slows down but continues reading
- The slower pace is maintained until the other reader gets back into the flow

It is critical to paired reading to continue the flow despite mistakes. 'Sounding out', etc. will negate the process because the purpose is to support comprehension by reducing the pressure on decoding. The level of comprehension after paired reading is often stunning.

I modelled paired reading with parent and child workshops and observed a boy who was struggling with decoding to such an extent that he was one word behind throughout the passage. Despite the fact that he seemed to be doing little more than 'parroting' the passage behind his parent, his comprehension was total and he answered a range of questions verbally with confidence and insight. The process of paired reading removed the barrier of decoding while enabling him to engage with the text at a high level of understanding. Although the decoding demands made the passage too hard for independent reading, paired reading included the student in the activity. This empowered him to comprehend at an ability appropriate level and he took great delight in his ability to answer questions correctly.

Paired reading offers a flexible response to reading challenges and can be used at any stage during a lesson, working well with fiction and non-fiction texts across the full range of genre and in any subject.

A word to the wise: If paired reading is introduced as an accommodation for students who are perceived to be poor readers, there may be a degree of stigmatization and corresponding resistance to its use.

Try introducing the process to stretch the most able and talented students, maybe challenging them to get to grips with material that would be far too hard if read independently. Once paired reading is used with all students it becomes part of house style and loses the stigma when also used with vulnerable students. The parental response to paired reading has been especially gratifying, with many parents reporting that the process has broken down barriers and, once again, they are reading with their children. Below are some guidelines for what I am calling 'social' paired reading, this is designed to rekindle a joy of reading by achieving 'purposeful success'.

The process begins with the child's choice of material, this is probably the key principle as it establishes the purpose for reading. All too often reading is something that is imposed on a child rather than stemming from curiosity, need or purpose. Spending time to find something that a child wants to read is important. It is important not to be too precious about subject matter, what we are trying to do is present reading as a purposeful, useful and fun activity. So, offering to pair read part of the Minecraft manual might work and graphic novels offer powerful visual cues to support the reading process. Pair reading anything with enthusiasm is better than struggling with conventional materials and approaches.

The final tip for parents in particular is to avoid dismissing some books as being 'too easy'. If reading is to be pleasurable it should be purposeful and fun, easy is good! Parents and teachers will find useful materials and a video from Education Scotland[2].

Ground Rules for 'Social' Paired Reading

- **Child's/student's choice** of material
- **Non-fiction is fine** - don't get precious over fiction, graphic novels work well, too.
- **Adult points to start** - if the reader can't manage a word, slow down, keep pointing. Definitely no TEACHING!
- **Relax, enjoy and have fun**

Reciprocal Teaching

The inclusive opportunities afforded by paired reading are enhanced when combined with reciprocal teaching. This takes the reading process up a level to engage with text as part of a group and offers opportunities to differentiate by task and/or outcome, depending on what is required. Reciprocal teaching is built around the five strategies used by effective readers to comprehend text. Much of the literature describes a four-stage process but I have included 'Reading' as stage 2. The stages are:

1. **Predicting** - effective readers begin by predicting the relevance of a text before reading. This acts as a filter to avoid wasting time on texts which may be irrelevant or lacking interest. The prediction process also creates a big picture about the content, allowing the reader to make use of a range of cues.

2. **Reading** – a range of ways to read a text which are directed by the students themselves

3. **Questioning** - asking questions helps the student to monitor and understand what is read

4. **Clarifying** – effective readers notice and stop when a word, phrase or passage does not make sense

5. **Summarising** – the discipline of going back to recall key ideas and points forms long term memories which can be recalled later

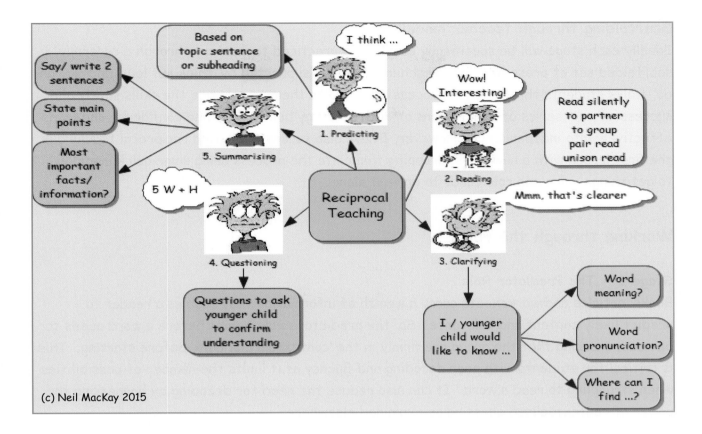

Each stage requires targetted teaching in order to develop a range of phase-specific skills. In this sense, there are parallels between reciprocal teaching and guided reading. However, the main difference is that reciprocal teaching is a group-based activity that can operate on real texts as they naturally occur across the full range of subjects and has the potential to include effective thinkers with currently weak decoding. There is also flexibility in the order in which the phases are used. Reading a mystery story encourages prediction throughout the piece, while a non-fiction passage may work better if summarised first using a range of contextual cues. Reciprocal teaching is an art as well as a science.

Making it work in the classroom

The power of reciprocal teaching lies in its ability to include, challenge and stretch a range of individuals in group settings, without the teacher always needing to give individual help. My preference is to set up groups or tables of students with a range of reading competencies. Ideally, each group has a mix of competent readers, strong decoders with weaker comprehension, quick thinking comprehenders who lack fluency and also students who struggle with both decoding and comprehension, in other words each group reflects the range of skills and competencies in the class. This is where reciprocal teaching becomes so effective, because it can engage all students in a common task and using the same materials, while offering opportunities for personalisation and differentiation as the lesson unfolds.

Scaffolding through teacher modelling

Ideally each stage will be specifically taught and practiced to mastery through a carefully scaffolded set of presentations. Teacher modelling, supported by 'think out loud' and 'say and do', walks students through each process and enables them to practice the skills safely and successfully. A series of mini lessons on each strategy builds skills and confidence and leads effectively into independence. However, I have also successfully used reciprocal teaching in the first lesson with a new class, dropping them into the process using some quick modelling to get things going and role cards to drive it along.

Working through the roles

Stage 1 - The Predictor Role

Books, articles and worksheets carry a wealth of information that enables a reader to predict likely content and relevance. So, the predictor's role begins before a word needs to be read, ensuring that the group are firmly in the 'contextual ball park' before starting. This is critical for students with poor decoding and fluency as it limits the number of possibilities when struggling to read a word. It can also reduce the need for decoding by harnessing the power of contextualised guessing as explained elsewhere.

The Predictor supports the group by using the TCP-QR process (Title, Captions, Picture, Questions, Reading) and asking:

i) Can you look at the title, captions and pictures to predict what the passage will be about?

ii) After reading the topic sentence of each paragraph, consider your predictions?

> **A word to the wise**: Reading the topic sentence and final sentence of each paragraph works even better and is also an excellent exam/test strategy for getting the big picture before reading.

iii) Having looked at everything so far, what do we predict this passage will be about?

iv) Please tell me your predictions so far.

Useful words and phrases to be modelled by teachers while talking through will include:

I wonder….	I think….
I suppose….	I imagine….
What I think might happen next….	
One prediction could be….	

These questions can be printed on role cards and also displayed on the working wall for easy reference. Properly done, the Predictor Role helps the group to set a purpose for reading and to monitor comprehension.

Stage 2 – The Reader Role

This role is not present in all models of reciprocal teaching but I think it is essential. The student with the reader role invites others to read in certain ways and up to certain points.

This is a perfect role for students with weak decoding as it enables them to allocate tasks without exposing any lack of competence or confidence. It also allows them to hear the passage, maybe participate in paired reading and so be ready to engage fully in the thinking opportunities that are to come. Adding the reader role adds a level of inclusivity, which is otherwise missing. The reader may need specific coaching to develop the language and strategies implicit within the role.

As before the language of this role will be presented on a card and ideally on the working wall as well. The purpose of the reading is to see if the predictions are correct. Appropriate reading tasks could include:

- Zane – please can you read the first 3 sentences/up to this point to the rest of us. Then please will Susie take over
- Please read the next bit to your partner
- Let's pair read the passage please
- Please can we all read the passage out loud, all together – ready?

The final task of the Reader Role is to lead a short discussion about the accuracy of predictions and to address any inaccuracies or misconceptions at this point.

Stage 3 – The Clarifier Role

By this point, all students, irrespective of the level of reading competence, should be able to interact fully with the gist of the text. Now it is time to drill down into meaning through the clarification process.

The Clarifier gives the group opportunities to identify any unfamiliar words, phrases, pronunciations and so on and to use the wisdom of the group to make them clear. Implicit within this process is the metacognitive responsibility to use 'self-help' strategies that are known to work. Using the context around a word or chunking to remove suffix and prefix will be helpful. Identifying words and phrases and inviting individuals to explain how to teach them to a younger child can also work really well.

Wise teachers may equip the Clarifier with a list of tricky elements for the group to unpack. The following prompts work well, either as open questions to the group or targeted at specific group members:

- Who can help me/a younger child understand the part where...?
- This word is tricky – can anyone help?
- How is this word pronounced?
- This phrase, sentence, chunk might not be clear to some people. Can anyone explain it?

The process of clarification adds an important problem solving process to reciprocal reading and makes it explicit. Students develop as strategic readers as they learn to identify and clarify difficult words or confusing, ambiguous chunks of text. The teacher can model a range of 'stuck strategies' which can be used when clarification is not immediate.

Talking through the process and then walking individuals, groups or the whole class through it supports the development of metacognitive strategies to be used when needed. Helpful strategies include:

- Miss out the word/phrase and read to the next full stop – or even read the following sentence to see if it helps
- Ask a neighbour
- Ask the group
- Ask the class expert – s/he may be wearing the mantle of the expert for a given activity
- Ask Wikipedia or Google

Stage 4 – The Questioner Role
Competent readers seem to ask themselves questions throughout the reading process. This implies a degree of automaticity in terms of decoding which frees the thinking process – formulating questions is not an easy task!

One of the benefits of reciprocal teaching is that it enables students who lack automaticity in this area to use the skills of the group to establish meaning. Because questioning is an integral part of the process students come to anticipate the need. Lubliner[3] goes further, suggesting that generating questions creates an automatic increase in comprehension. Experience shows that when students are challenged to 'play the teacher' they stretch their understanding of both detail and the big picture. A good place to start is always through the '5W and H' questions:

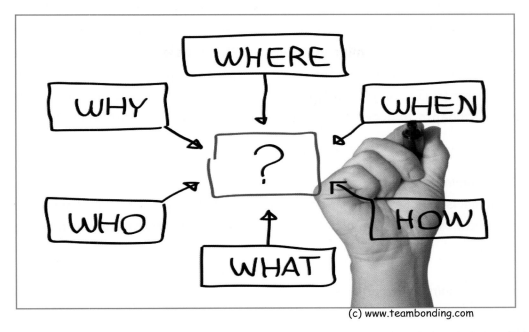

One of the challenges is to support students to break free from asking predictable 'on the lines' questions. I encourage my students to avoid asking questions that can be answered by 'cut and paste', by identifying a phrase or sentence from the text and copying it. Questions that generate cut and paste answers require lower order thinking skills (LOTS) and neither formulating them or answering them will provide appropriate stretch and challenge. A simple solution is to provide the Questioner with question stems, which will automatically result in higher order thinking skills (HOTS).

The following question stems, aimed specifically at HOTS, can be used for either evaluation or analysis:

- Is there a better solution to ...?
- Judge the value of ...
- Can you defend your position about ...?
- Do you think ... is a good or a bad thing?
- How would you have handled ...?
- What changes to ... would you recommend?
- Do you believe?
- Are you a ... person?
- How would you feel if ...?
- How effective are ...?
- What do you think about ...?

See also the Blooms Taxonomy list on page 73.

It is also worth demonstrating to students how the word 'might' adds power and HOTS to almost every question as it automatically demands open ended thinking. A question like "What is the impact of global warming in Antarctica?" invites students to cut and paste from the text. But asking "What might be the impact?" opens up opportunities for inference, prediction and other HOTS. Coincidentally, the concepts of inference and prediction are often easier for students to access through writing questions than answering them.

Stage 5 - The Summariser Role
The role of Summariser is key to the whole process as s/he asks group members to sift through all the detail to recall and order the key points. Effective summary tasks for the summariser include:

- State the main points of this ....
- Summarise the passage in two sentences
- What are the 5 most important points
- Use the plan below to summarise the passage
- What would this character/that person consider as the main points?

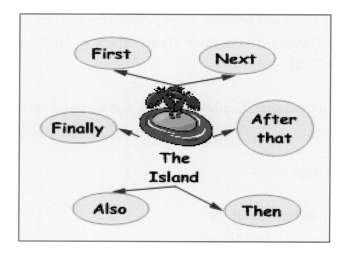

Summary questions which require cut and paste, 'on the lines' thinking obviously have a place but they will not provide challenge and stretch for quick thinking, slow decoding students. However, equipping the Summariser with synthesis question stems has the potential to take the questioning process to another, quite demanding level. Synthesis is about going 'beyond the lines' to see the passage in a new way.

A summary question such as "Explain why the planet Venus is unsuitable for habitation", is asking for an analysis, selection and ordering of key points for a LOTS answer. Asking "What improvements in current technology would be required for a successful landing on Venus?" is asking for HOTS, requiring students to go through the summary process to marshall key points and then go beyond it to synthesise an answer using inference and prediction.

The summary also lends itself to light hearted responses – my current favourites include challenging students to respond in the form of a tweet (a message of up to 140 characters including spaces) or a haiku. This form of Japanese poetry is made up of three lines, the first line having 5 syllables, the second having 7 syllables and the third having 5 syllables. This syllable pattern of '5-7-5' can produce some remarkable insights in a very compact form.

The summary process, which requires students to condense a passage into the important elements, can place significant demands on working memory. A 'memory lite' solution involves the use of post-it notes as part of a group or pair brainstorm. This activity can be stipulated by the teacher as the final summary task before moving on. The instructions can be on the table and/or on the working wall and either led by the Summariser or as a whole class activity.

A set of excellent role cards are available as a free download from **http://www.adrianbruce.com**

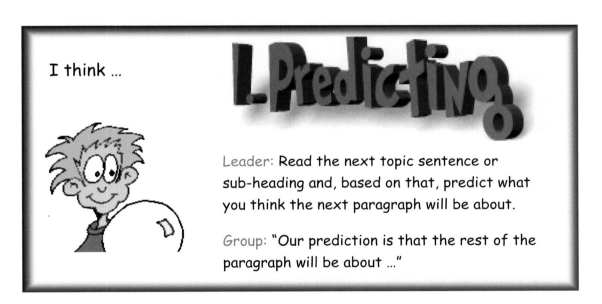

Also there is a wealth of free resources and materials available on the TES Resources website: **www.TES.co.uk/teaching-resources**. Many of these resources are excellent and include prompt cards and lists of questions.

Recap

Issue 7 for Total Teaching is:

How do I include quick thinking, slow decoders in comprehension activities?

The Total Teaching solution is:

To include vulnerable students through paired reading and reciprocal teaching.

by:

- Using guided reading but be aware of the risk of disengaging quick thinking, slow decoders
- Using paired reading – it can solve the problem identified above. Introduce with strong readers first
- Using reciprocal teaching – it works really well to include priority learners
- Taking time to teach the roles
- Investing time to support students to ask HOT questions – scaffold by providing HOT question stems

References

1. **J M Burkins and M M Croft, Preventing misguided reading: New strategies for guided reading teachers**
   International Reading Association, Newark, 2010

2. **Education Scotland, Paired Reading in Action: a video**
   http://www.educationscotland.gov.uk/video/s/kingspark.asp?

3. **Shira Lubiner, A practical guide to reciprocal teaching**
   McGraw Hill, 2001

Chapter 10

Reluctant Writers

Issue 8: My students can usually tell a good story but their writing rarely matches the quality of their ideas and expression

Getting reluctant writers to write

Most teachers know that moment when, after preparing a class for writing and setting them off, a significant proportion of students are still staring into space. While it is easy to assume that this is because the students still do not have any ideas, my experience suggests that this is actually not the case.

These problems touch all learning needs and are especially common among some of our brightest boys. The techniques described below have proved effective across a range of genre, age group, motivation and belief. The feedback I get from teachers when modelling these techniques is that many students produce the best writing they have done that year.

The strategy pulls together some important principles:

- Students need the big picture and examples of good work before they start
- Keys to success include thorough teacher modelling and self-talk and, in the early stages at least, micro-managing the process through direct teaching

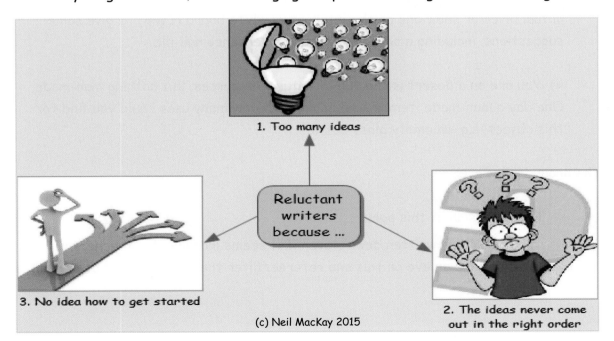

1. Too many ideas

Reluctant writers because ...

3. No idea how to get started

2. The ideas never come out in the right order

(c) Neil MacKay 2015

The three main problems are:

- Too many ideas
- The ideas do not come out in the order in which they are needed
- The students have no idea how to get started

As a basic principle it is important to emphasise to students that we value all ideas – though we will inevitably value some more than others. So acknowledging all ideas with respect is positive, even if they are initially unhelpful and/or inappropriate. A simple "thank you" and then moving swiftly on works well with some of the more outlandish/inappropriate responses!

The best way I know of getting ideas out, in any subject and any genre, is to use 'post-it note brainstorming', either after some form of introduction or as a starting point. I prefer to organise my class into mixed ability groups. Although some primary schools in the UK establish Kagan Groups and these work well for this activity. I prefer to introduce the principle of post-it note brainstorming as a fun activity before using it for the task in hand.

a) Appoint a scribe for each group, preferably the quickest, neatest writer. This is why it is important to have students with a mix of ability, ideas, basic skills, etc. around each table. The scribe is responsible for recording group ideas on small post-it notes, one idea per post-it

b) Set the class a problem. Group members tell their scribe their ideas and the scribe then writes each idea on a post-it and sticks it on the table.

My favourite scenarios are:

i) How many uses can you think of for one house brick? It helps to have an actual brick or show one on the interactive white board (IWB). I give some suggestions, including a paper weight and emergency nail file

ii) You are on a desert island full of natural resources, but nothing man-made. One day a man-made item is washed ashore. How many uses could you find for this object, e.g. an empty glass bottle?

The ground rules are:

- No discussion at this point
- What is said is written down – even if it seems irrelevant - teachers will need to keep an eye on this and referee/filter the contributions of certain individuals

c) After 60 seconds ask for a count up of ideas and issue the 'originality challenge' which works like this:

    i) Each group selects 3 ideas which are so amazingly original (crazy?) that no other group could possibly have thought of them

    ii) Sequence them on the table – most original first

    iii) One by one, ask the groups for their most original idea and see if other groups have the same idea. If they do, the group can try ideas 2 and 3. The aim is to have one original idea and it is rare for a group not to be successful.

The purpose of this activity is to establish the principle of thinking without boundaries and then to develop the core activities of selecting and ordering ideas and information. It takes about 10 minutes or so, depending on the age group. Sometimes I will do both activities if I feel that the process needs to be practiced.

A word of warning, this is a noisy and high-energy session so be prepared to cope with it. Interestingly, groups seem to settle down quickly for the next task, despite becoming very animated during the initial brainstorming process. Having established and practiced post-it brainstorming it is now ready for use in any subject and in any genre. I have used it successfully in Science to dump all the ideas about an experiment showing the effect of salt on ice; in Geography to prepare writing on global warming issues; in History to write a report on an aspect of World War 2; and in English to prepare everything from fiction through book reports to discursive.

We can now apply this technique to two writing styles, narrative into fiction and discursive, with the addition of a new element, which is to invite students to draw first. For years I have used drawing as a carrot, as the reward for finishing, but I now believe that drawing helps a majority of students build that all important big picture.

So the sequence recommended is:

    i)   Draw – to fix the big picture
    ii)   Brainstorm - to get the ideas out
    iii)   Select - according to the criteria or rubric
    iv)   Order – for effective sequencing of ideas
    v)   Re-process and add value - into an appropriate form of alternative evidence, which could be a mind-map, flow-chart, story-board, labelled diagram, etc.
    vi)   Talk it – to add more value and go for flow
    vii)   Write it

Below is a framework/scaffold from an excellent UK website: **www.primarytexts.co.uk**:

To plan a story set in an imaginary world

Draw and describe your fantasy setting.	Draw and describe your fantasy creatures.
_____ _____ _____	_____ _____ _____

Useful words: brown black grey red orange blue green white silver gold eyes sky tree mountain castle clouds evil horrible old cold hot warm rainy snow leaves beautiful pretty flowers skin nose hair arms legs head small tall big fur scales ugly scary smelly enormous dragon monster animal witch wizard dwarf giant

(c) www.primarytexts.co.uk

The student is invited to 'draw and describe' and I tend to ask for both, in whatever order a student prefers. I struggle to visualise but words trigger pictures for me, so writing first leads me to create the picture in my head. Other students see the picture in their mind's eye and use this as the basis for writing.

So starting by drawing and labelling a picture of the experiment, the impact of a tsunami and so on, can have a significant impact on the ability of many students to crystallise their thinking.

A word to the wise about drawing: Some students will try to spend all lesson on the drawing in order to avoid writing especially those who lack confidence in their ability to write. Using a sand timer or other timer set for, say, two minutes gives them just enough time for their drawing. The deal is that once the sand runs out/the bell rings, it is time to stop drawing and start writing.

124

Now it is time for post-it brainstorming, as outlined above, together with the selection and ordering process. 'Going for 5' seems to work in terms of how many post-it notes to select for a paragraph, so the process finishes with 5 or 6 post-it notes stuck on the table in the most appropriate order.

One of the most positive features of working this way is that the order can be reworked without requiring anything to be crossed out. The message is that this is still a fluid situation and it is evolving all the time. Finally I give a sentence to kick start the writing. There is no obligation to use my sentence but it is there if needed.

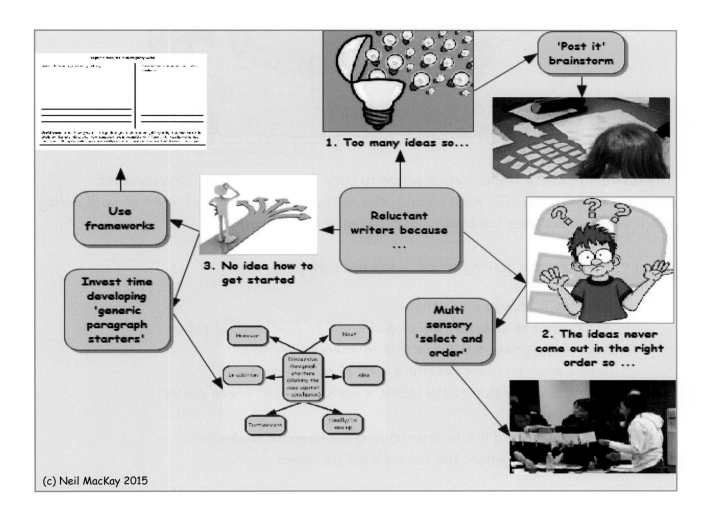

Treasure Island Writing Task – narrative into fiction

(c) Dutch Rennaissance Press LLC

The task is to draw an island, decide where to bury the treasure and plan a series of adventures on the way. For most classes, this will be the culmination of a unit of work during which language and ideas will have been explored at great length.

My language to set the activity tends to follow a script:

- Each table, choose your artist
- Artist draw an interestingly shaped island on your piece of paper
- Rest of the group, make sure it is an interesting shape
- Draw a small treasure chest in a good place to hide it
- On the opposite side of the island, x marks the spot where you will come ashore
- Now use a dotted line to draw an interesting route from where you come ashore to where the treasure will be buried

A word to the wise: I am not asking for features, mountains, etc. to be added at this stage. But some students will not be able to help themselves! If you see it ask them to wait, the time will come!

It is nearly time for the post-it brainstorm. First ask the artist to turn the map over for now, this is important. Each group appoints a scribe who can write quickly and neatly.

The focus of the brainstorm is:

"What interesting features on an island would you expect to encounter on your journey from the shore to where you will bury the treasure?"

I always use a slide show with pictures of a volcano, hills, waterfall, forest, ruins, swamp monster, etc. to stimulate the imagination. The scribe's job is to write nouns on separate post-it notes as the group shout out their ideas. 'Nouns only' is the rule. Keep the brainstorm going until each group has at least 6-10 features.

Now it is time to select and order. choose the 5 most interesting or potentially exciting features and stick them on the table in the best order in which to encounter them. Next, turn the map over and stick the features onto the route drawn on the map – this turns the route into a time line.

In this example, the features have been drawn on. This will definitely happen with some groups and is not a problem, as long as it does not take too long. The important process is selecting and ordering. It is time to add some value. Currently each feature is identified by a noun. Now we need at least one adjective to describe each noun. This is a good time to throw in some challenges:

> "Who can use an adjective to show alliteration, and/or personification?"
>
> "Can you show me one example of simile to describe a feature?"
>
> ....etc.

I find it better to drop challenges in while they are working rather than expecting them to refer back to lesson outcomes.

At this point we have an island with a route, along which are well-described features, the narrative is completed. Now it is time for some fiction.

The overall aim of the activity is to get individual pieces of work which are influenced and stimulated by the group task and I could say, "Go and write up your journey across the island". But this would immediately intimidate my reluctant writers and miss a golden opportunity to add even more value before we start writing. The jewel in the crown of this activity is to say:

"As a group, tell out loud all the adventures you had from landing on the island and following the route, to burying the treasure."

Your starter sentence could be:

"We crawled up the beach and....."

I want them to point their way from post-it to post-it and to describe their adventure. They can add any words as they go along, and change anything they wish to make the narrative more effective. Some groups even decide to replace some nouns and re-work the adjectives correspondingly.

This 'talk phase' is critical to the ultimate flow of the written piece. Some groups are overly organised and polite and allocate different post-its to each other. This can also happen when a Teaching Assistant or Teacher Aide feels uncomfortable in what is quite a fluid situation and tries to create a structure. In practice, this is too formal and the process seems to work much better when it is organic, noisy and just teetering on the creative side of organised chaos.

Now we are ready to write. Beginning with title, date, etc. will kill the momentum built up – the whole class are desperate to start writing at this point. One solution is to ensure that the title, date, learning outcome and starter sentence are already written up in the students' books so they can start writing immediately. Alternatively there is no reason why we cannot leave a few lines for the title and then get stuck into the writing.

An accommodation for some students will be to give them paper with the starter sentence already written, now they can choose to carry it on or ignore it and start in their own way. Whatever they choose to do, having a starter sentence invariably seems to get them writing more quickly. The picture below is from a different writing task but the principle of giving a starter sentence ensures that this occasionally reluctant writer has started with confidence.

What I am looking for is every student to start writing immediately – and most do. I often launch the writing with 'Ready, steady, go!' Those who still have not started are usually trying too hard to think of an original opening sentence, which is laudable, if misguided. I pick them off one by one by asking each student two questions:

1. "What do you want to say to start this?" They are usually locked into unhelpful self-talk at this point so asking them to say what they are thinking of out loud can be a powerful trigger

2. "May I write it in for you?" Most students find it helpful if we write that opening sentence or two which they will dictate. Then they seem to be back in the flow.

Pie Corbett[2] identifies three stages in writing: imitation, innovation and independent application. The above way of developing writing seems to generate similar levels across the range of writers. The best writers in the group are stimulated by the pre-writing tasks but usually go their own way to work independently and innovate. Other writers find the framework in front of them helpful because it gives them 'headroom' to add value, they invent extra aspects as their stories develop. But is the reluctant writers who tend to make the most progress as they confidently imitate the group story, using the route on the map as a time line to organise their own writing.

Myth busting

Myth 1: "If we write a starter sentence for one, they will all expect it"
Occasionally I am challenged about my willingness to provide opening sentences by teachers who are worried that, if they do it for one, everyone will expect it. All I say is that this has never happened to me. Most students in the class have already started writing and are so focussed by this point that they have no ears for anything other than their inner voice.

If, by some chance, there is an outbreak of 'learned helplessness' among a majority of students who are asking for support, this would suggest that the process has not been properly embedded or perhaps was rushed. The process as described above works precisely because it takes time – and time invested now pays off when students become independent writers and get started very quickly in the future.

Myth 2: "This support is really rewarding lazy students"
Once again this does not seem to be the case – they are generally not lazy, just stuck. When kick started, these students rarely stop and go on to write at considerable length.

Myth 3: "I haven't got time to write starter sentences for some when I've got the whole class to attend to."
There are two points to make here:

> i. If the activity has been introduced and developed properly, the rest of the class have no need of the teacher – they are focussed, on task and writing at length

> ii. The cost of failing to accommodate stuck learners is often simmering and then bubbling disruption.

I am frequently surprised when teachers tell me that they have not got the time to personalise in this way - yet they do seem to have the time to spend grumbling at students who are off task.

The 'shout, stick , select and order, talk, write' way of organising ideas works well for writing styles which require a loose scaffold or framework and is perfect for fiction and the "Imagine you are…." tasks in Humanities, Social Studies and similar areas. It can also work when something more structured is required because the same principles underpin expository writing work across the curriculum.

Building in the power of 'Slow writing'

David Didau[3], the creator of Slow writing explains the concept:

> "I first came up with the idea when teaching an intervention class of Year 11, grade C/D borderline boys in about 2008. Broadly speaking they were willing, but no matter what I tried the writing they produced was leaden, plodding stuff."

> "I gave them all kinds of outlandish and creative prompts which they would dead bat and produce yet another dreary yawnfest. Needless to say, we were all getting a bit irritated with each other. Out of sheer frustration I decide to give them explicit instructions on how to write a text sentence by sentence."

Sort of like this:

- *Your first sentence must start with a present participle (that's a verb ending in 'ing')*
- *Your second sentence must contain only three words.*
- *Your third sentence must contain a semi-colon*
- *Your fourth sentence must be a rhetorical question*
- *Your fifth sentence will start with an adverb*
- *Your sixth sentence will be 22 words exactly*

I have taken these ideas, which work superbly well as described above, and created the 'Flip the clip' activity which places students in charge of the challenges. It works like this:

- The 'flip the clip' templates are prepared and shared out within each group
- At appropriate intervals during a writing task the teacher calls "flip the clip!"
- A student places a large paper clip on the template and uses a pencil to make a spinner
- S/he flips the clip and the next sentence starter is determined by the position of the clip.
- If it lands on a previously used starter, flip again

The students seem to appreciate the random nature of the challenge and enjoy hearing the groans from their peers when they land on one of the more tricky starters.

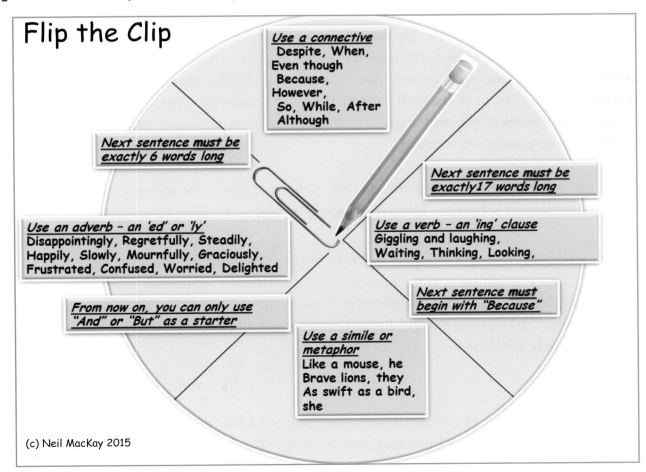

Flip the Clip

Use a connective
Despite, When, Even though Because, However, So, While, After Although

Next sentence must be exactly 6 words long

Next sentence must be exactly 17 words long

Use an adverb – an 'ed' or 'ly'
Disappointingly, Regretfully, Steadily, Happily, Slowly, Mournfully, Graciously, Frustrated, Confused, Worried, Delighted

Use a verb – an 'ing' clause
Giggling and laughing, Waiting, Thinking, Looking,

From now on, you can only use "And" or "But" as a starter

Next sentence must begin with "Because"

Use a simile or metaphor
Like a mouse, he Brave lions, they As swift as a bird, she

Expository Writing

This type of writing is used to explain, describe, give information, or inform. It is probably the main type of writing used in school and, for this reason, I continue to be surprised at the amount of time dedicated to writing fiction at the expense of other, more commonly used forms of writing.

While I am aware that many may disagree with me with regard to the value of fiction writing it is, by definition, implicit and abstract, two unhelpful attributes for reluctant writers in general and Dyslexic writers in particular. On the other hand, the formulaic process of writing exposition can, as shown below, become the basis for effective fiction.

For exposition the text is organized around one topic and developed according to a pattern. The writer of an expository text cannot assume that the reader or listener has prior knowledge or prior understanding of the topic that is being discussed and, since clarity requires strong organization, one of the most important mechanisms to improve skills in exposition is to improve the organisation of the text.

The power of exposition as a Total Teaching writing tool is the way it blends the three Zones – the D Zone, the A Zone and the AD Zone – to create the finished piece. Each Zone has a particular contribution to make to the process and it pushes students to work out of perceived comfort zones for part of the time, in the certain knowledge that more preferred ways of working are just around the corner. I find it helpful to warn students when part of a task may be 'uncomfortable' for some by referring to their preferred ways of working. This honours the 'no surprises' principle that works well with students on the ASD and ADHD Spectrums and also serves to validate and legitimise individual preferences. Pointing out to individuals that the next task will not suit them but reassuring them that it will come to an end and be followed by something less challenging is, in my opinion at least, no more than common courtesy and good teaching.

This is the way I teach 'exposition into fiction'. Once mastered, the process transfers to most genre and most subjects. I find it especially effective for discursive writing.

> **A word to the wise:** What follows takes far longer to describe that to actually organise in the classroom. Once the core principles have been embedded the students accelerate. Time invested in getting the planning and process right for paragraph 1 is repaid as students are empowered to engage in independent learning.

I introduce the concept of exposition with examples and I find the passage below to be very useful as a "Can you work out the Exposition Formula or Rule" challenge:

Essay Title	Fang the Frogilator
Paragraph 1 - Introduction	
Topic sentence (main idea)	My pet is a cross between a frog and an alligator and is a very difficult pet.
Example sentence 1 (sub topic)	He is very ugly and difficult to look after.
Example sentence 2 (sub topic)	Playing with him is exciting, but can be very dangerous.
Example sentence 3 (sub topic)	He thinks he takes care of me but I am losing a lot of friends.
Concluding sentence (repeating main idea)	So you can see a Frogilator is a tricky pet to keep.
Paragraph 2	
Synonym topic sentence from Introduction	Fang is a strange multi-coloured creature and he is a bit of a challenge.
Example sentence 1 (supporting the topic)	His skins looks like green scales and he is covered in bumpy, pointed spots.
Example sentence 2 (supporting the topic)	The main problem is he cannot decide if he wants to live under a stone or in a pond.
Example sentence 3 (supporting the topic)	When he swims he forgets that he cannot breathe underwater and he sinks.
Concluding sentence (repeating main idea)	However it is dangerous to give a frogilater the kiss of life.
Paragraph 3	
Synonym topic sentence from Introduction	Fang is fun to play with but it is a risky business.
Example sentence 1 (supporting the topic)	He has teeth like an alligator but, because he is part frog, he has a long tongue which keeps getting tangled up with his teeth.
Example sentence 2 (supporting the topic)	Fang chews everything and he can bite his way through most things so I wear special gloves to play with him.
Example sentence 3 (supporting the topic)	We took Fang to the local swimming pool once but it was a big mistake because he kept biting holes in children's arm bands.
Concluding sentence (repeating main idea)	I told him to stop, but he cannot hear when his ears are full of water.

Paragraph 4	
Synonym topic sentence from Introduction	A Frogilator is a very loyal and faithful pet but he can be agressive, especially if he thinks people are threatening me.
Example sentence 1 (supporting the topic)	When I play fighting games with my friends Fang goes crazy and tries to bite holes in their shoes and I have to buy new ones from my pocket money.
Example sentence 2 (supporting the topic)	Sometimes my friends try to pick him up but he always bites them.
Example sentence 3 (supporting the topic)	He doesn't always know when to stop biting.
Concluding sentence (repeating main idea)	Now my friends have stopped coming round to play.
Paragraph 5 - Conclusion	
Topic sentence from main idea	As you can see a Frogilator is a tricky pet to keep.
Synonym sentence from para 2	It takes a great deal of time and attention making sure Fang is a happy creature and he will definitely not win any beauty contests.
Synonym sentence from para 3	Fang is fun to play with but his sharp teeth mean that this can be a risky business.
Synonym sentence from para 4	A Frogilator is always possessive and causes problems when my friends come round to play.
Concluding sentence (repeating main idea)	Fang is definitely a labour of love, but as they say, a Frogilator is for life, not just for Christmas.

This works well in small groups with one copy to each group and I prefer to ask groups to report back to me quietly rather than to the whole class. This simple piece of assessment for learning enables me to monitor what is happening, maybe to add a supplementary task for a group that has solved the problem and ensures that, when the answers are shared, they are correct.

As I go from group to group there are always one or two individuals who have really understood the task and have explained it well to me. I invite them to report back to the whole class in a minute or two, but always give the opportunity to refuse. In practice most students enjoy feeding back if they have had time to think. I will quite deliberately ask some of my vulnerable learners to report back but I always give them time to rehearse their feedback to me and then to their group before I put them on the spot. A small investment of time like this pays off in terms of the feedback being precise and to the point.

The principle we are looking for is:

The second sentence in paragraph 1 is modified to start paragraph 2
The third sentence in pargraph 1 is modified to start pargraph 3
The fourth sentence in paragraph 1 is modified to start paragraph 4
....etc.

This principle defines expository writing and is easy to use following the 'shout, stick, select and order, talk, write' process described earlier. It can work like this:

The task is to write an expository piece on the book 'Total Teaching'. Using the post-it brainstorming technique, generate ideas about the main messages of the book and then select and order to choose 4-5 main ideas.

1. The importance of the 'just enough' skill set
2. Think preference not problem
3. The importance of 'memory lite'
4. Getting it right for priority learners gets it right for all

Paragraph 1 combines points 1-4 into an introduction:

i) Vulnerable students learn better when their class teachers have 'just enough' of the skills of a specialist

ii) It is very helpful to view the learning needs of students with ASD, ADHD and Dyslexia as preferred ways of learning rather than automatically as problems

iii) Many of the learning issues presented by vulnerable students can be due to problems with working memory

iv) We find that fine tuning lessons to get it right for priority learners actually gets it right for all students in the class

Paragraph 2 will be about preferred ways of learning and will start with a 'synonym version' (same ideas using different words) of sentence 2.

Although vulnerable students may find it difficult to learn certain aspects, taking time to find out out how they prefer to learn can minimise many problems. For example......

Paragraph 3 will be about the importance of assessing and reducing memory loads and will start with a synonym version of sentence 3.

Limitations in working memory can cause significant problems in following instructions and generally keeping up with a lesson. Analysing storage and processing demands....

Paragraph 4 will be about whole class benefits with a 'notice and adjust' approach:

As teachers gain in confidence and awareness they become more able to adapt lessons quickly in response to differences in the way individuals respond to various tasks. As a result....

If desired, Paragraph 5 could repeat all the points made in paragraph 1 but in a different way.

Discursive and Argument/Opinion writing using the exposition model

This model works well for expressing opinions and writing a balanced argument.

Applying the formula and process to a balanced argument is simply a case of:

1. Student research into a topic
2. Post-it brainstorming for ideas - both for and against

And then – making the case 'for':

3. Basic ordering of ideas (BOI) on flow-chart for topic sentences of post-it ideas
4. Write paragraph 1 from the BOI topics
5. Develop further paragraphs from the BOI topic sentences in paragraph 1

Good paragraph starter captions include:

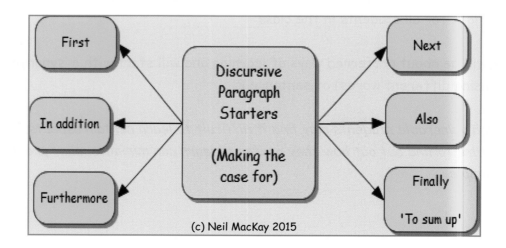

Then repeat stages 3-5 to make the case 'against' using a selction of captions as above, but probably starting with 'However'

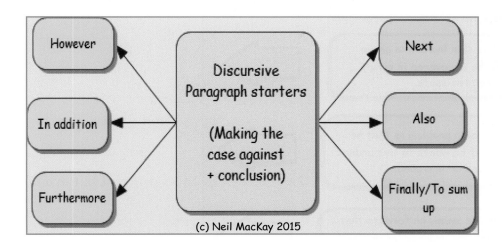

Sue Palmer's books will be well known to primary teachers in the UK and they are unreservedly recommended for all students, especially secondary.   The writing process is explained visually through a series of scaffolds which work extremely well and I particularly like her 'Persuasion Book'. Combining her persuasion framework with my formula for exposition creates a powerful model for extending writing which is especially appropriate for older students.

Here is a worked example of a persuasive piece based on the pros and cons of keeping an imaginary pet, in this case a cross between an frog and an alligator, called a frogilator.

Fang the Frogilator

First the student lists out 5 key points about Frogilators.

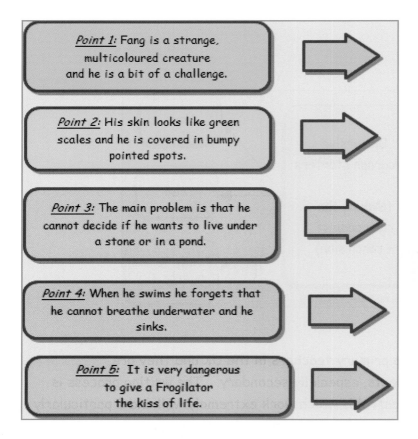

Then the student elborates on the 5 key points by adding 3 related points about Frogilators.

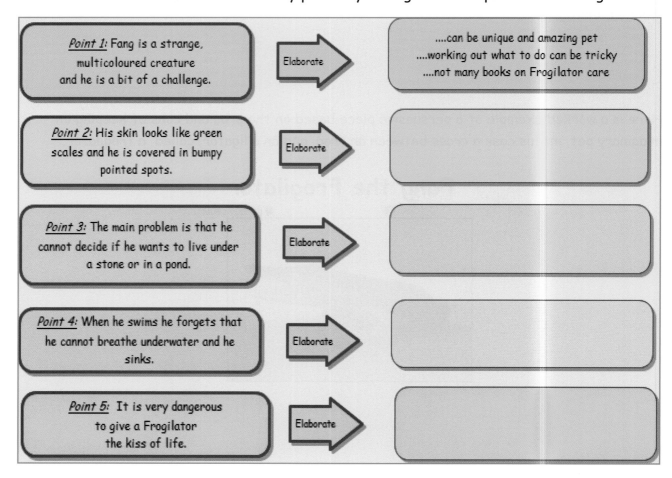

From Persuasive to Discursive

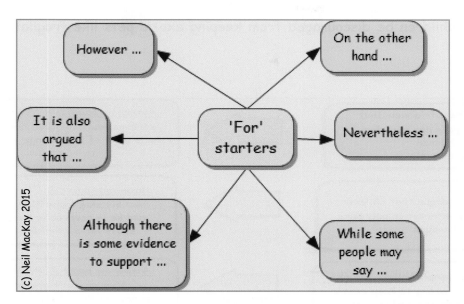

Having persuaded the reader that a frogilator is a good pet, we have the opportunity to stay with the overall format and extend the piece into a discussion. For this piece the writer can use a modified version of the persuasive piece above as the second part of a discursive essay to justify keeping exotic creatures as pets.

The key is to present an argument in a balanced way so that the reader can appreciate the arguments both for and against the position. At the end the writer will state the final opinion.

Using an already prepared persuasive piece as part of the discussion emphasises the point about transfer of skills and also, once again, keeps the process as explicit as possible.

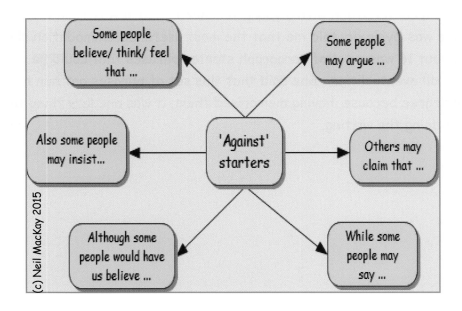

Opening statement:

"Should children be discouraged from keeping exotic pets like frogilators?"

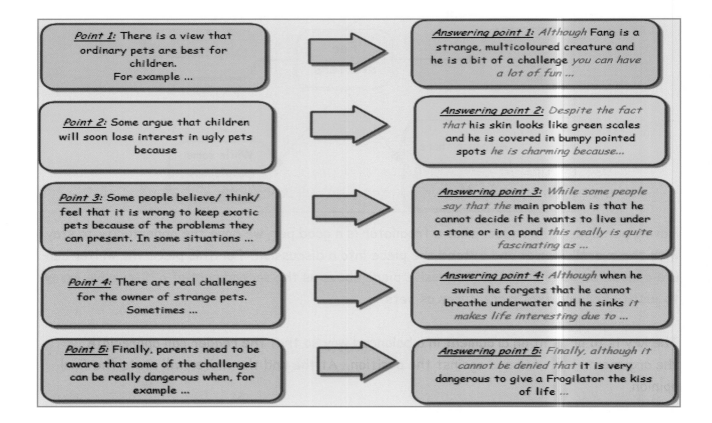

While this is, at best, a formulaic, very pragmatic, no frills way of approaching persuasion and argument/opinion it enables students to earn much needed marks in internal assessments and public exams.

I am reminded of a conversation with a young teacher in South Australia who, while sharing with me that she was Dyslexic, told me that the most useful accommodation she was given when she was about 16 was a set of paragraph starter phrases that could be used time and again for almost all eventualities. She said that this set of phrases got her through public exams and her degree because, having memorised them, it was one less thing to think about when it came to doing the writing.

Recap

Issue 8 for Total Teaching is:

> My students can usually tell a good story or essay
> but their writing rarely matches
> the quality of ideas and expression

The Total Teaching solution is:

> to use groups to develop ideas and process writing
> in a staged approach using kinaesthetic strategies.

by:

- Setting the big picture – pictures work well
- Using post-it notes and scribing to follow the 'shout, stick, select, order' process
- Building up the quality in layers – nouns, then adjectives, then connectives, etc.
- Using group talk before writing
- Always offering paragraph starters

References

1. **Kagan Groups,** See www.kaganonline.com

2. **Pie Corbett,** See www.talkforwriting.co.uk

3. **David Didau, The Learning Spy**
   http://www.learningspy.co.uk/english-gcse/how-to-improve-writing/

Chapter 11

We need to talk about Gavin, - a case study

Total Teaching solutions for stuck pupils

Gavin is 10 and he is stuck. Every day he drags himself to school knowing that the ideas in his head will never get onto paper and his inaccurate reading and spelling will put him under pressure again and again. Although he is currently well behaved he is beginning to think that, if he cannot be good, he might as well be bad and, as we will find out shortly, he could be very, very good at being bad, if he put his mind to it.

To compound matters Gavin's school is successful but also rather traditional and at the moment, seems to value neat presentation, punctuation and accurate reading and spelling above more alternative evidence of achievement. As a result his often insightful comments and observations in class are not really valued because he cannot seem to turn them into 'markable' sentences and paragraphs despite, in the eyes of his class teacher, having some ability.

Following a rather tense interview with his parents about Gavin's lack of progress, the SENCO decided to assess Gavin using the LASS programme from Lucid[1]. The results are shown below and the profile indicates quite clearly that, although Gavin's basic skills are extremely weak, his reasoning score suggests him to be one of the brighter boys in the school. The problem is that he is currently in a special needs group for most of his time in class and is being taught at a slower pace, effectively treated as a slow learner. Now Gavin is many things, but a slow learner he is not. Actually, he is a 'think faster' pupil with a clear gap between the levels he achieves when assessed traditionally and what he could score if he had a reader and a scribe.

What's going on here?

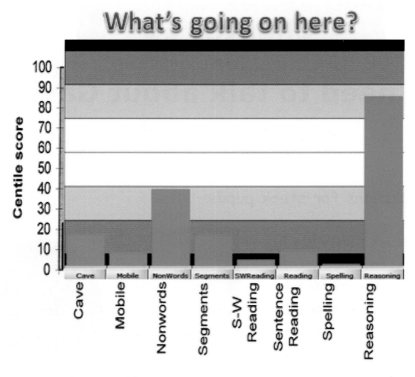

(c) LUCID Research

Looking at Gavin's profile more closely it becomes apparent that his basic skills are below the 40th centile, 60% of children of his age will score more highly. His visual spatial memory (Cave) and auditory sequential memory (Mobile) are particularly weak, explaining in part why Gavin finds it so difficult to decode words to read and encode them to spell.

Gavin does have some word attack skills, indicated by his performance on non-words, but he clearly finds it especially difficult to apply them to segmenting and reading single words and sentences. His very low spelling score will also fail to surprise and his poor performance at these attainment and diagnostic items is the reason that the school placed him on the special needs table.

Now the school has a new problem to address. Gavin is now recognised as one of the brighter pupils in the school and clearly needs to be grouped with his 'ability peers' in order to develop and stretch his cognition. At the same time he needs to be supported with the basic access skills of literacy.

Also, while there is no money available to put in any more support, Gavin's parents are now pushing hard to ensure that he is empowered to achieve at an ability appropriate level.

Fortunately the SENCO recently read the report of the Sutton Trust on the way the pupil premium was being spent. The Sutton Report concluded that, while 1:1 and small group placements were 'low impact for high cost' interventions, the following whole class approaches impacted extremely well on the achievement of vulnerable learners like Gavin:

- Effective feedback
- Metacognition and self-regulation strategies
- Peer tutoring/peer assisted learning

Time for Total Teaching

The time is right to move the focus away from Gavin and to explore how his class teacher can be empowered to develop the skills of a Total Teacher. Specifically to develop 'just enough' skills of a SENCO or Higher Level TA (HLTA) to work with and around his basic skill issues. At the same time there is an imperative to include him in whole class activities by tweaking assessment for learning and opportunities to present alternative evidence of achievement.

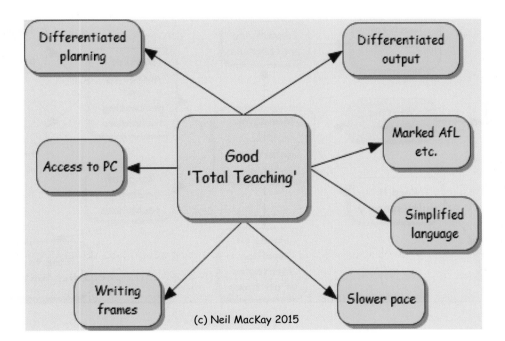

(c) Neil MacKay 2015

Gavin needs to sit at an appropriate table for the thinking and group work challenges and maybe move back to support for some of the reading and writing. The final Total Teaching challenge is to recognise that the only element in a classroom that can be changed quickly is the teacher's approaches, methods, materials and responses which require a number of paradigm shifts.

Total Teaching and reasonable classroom adjustments

1. Gavin's working memory 'quick fix' – leave it on the board longer!
Pupils like Gavin may score poorly on tests of reading accuracy and spelling and, in consequence, may be perceived as lacking phonological awareness. In practice many of them will actually have appropriate awareness. They just cannot remember the sounds, the patterns or the sequences. If these issues are related to working memory, a failure to blend c/a/t may be more indicative of a failure in remembering, processing and presenting three sounds rather than a phonological problem.

Dr. Tracy Alloway[2] is quite clear:

> *"working memory skills……… at 5 years old were the best predictor*
> *of reading, spelling and maths outcomes six years later."*

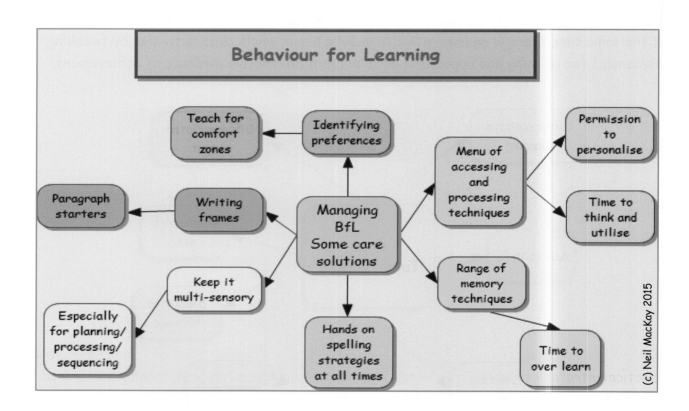

Looking back over a long career as a very enthusiastic teacher of phonics, I wonder how many children I have subjected to a rather knee jerk 'death by phonics' approach at KS2 and beyond, when what they really needed was support to develop working memory?

Effective responses include using the sound box techniques from Letters and Sounds and/or plastic letters to maintain that essential kinaesthetic element which can be so easily marginalised. Dr Alloway sensibly suggests employing strategies to reduce memory demand alongside what she calls "adaptive working memory training" such as Jungle Memory[3].

If we ask Gavin, he will tell us that we take material off the screen too quickly. An effective response is to ensure that there is at least one white board, next to the screen and preferably two. The teacher fills the screen and then moves to the white board, leaving the screen information available to be re-visited. Moving next maybe to another board or a flip chart, the teacher ensures that two screens of information, advice, strategy, etc. are always available to support those with currently weak working memory.

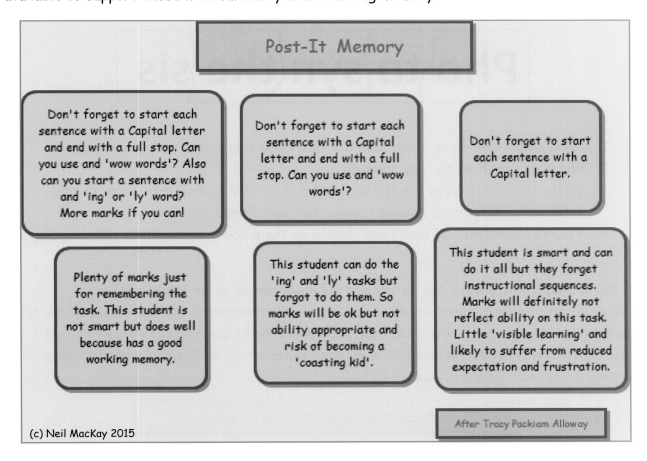

Put alongside more effective chunking of information and instructions and simplified language – not over simplified, just simple enough, Gavin's issues with working memory can cease to be such a barrier. This is especially the case when he is clear about how he prefers to receive, process and present information and uses a metacognitive menu of tried, tested and practiced strategies. Then Gavin needs 'permission to personalise' from teachers prepared to require and mark alternative evidence of achievement.

2 . Hands on spelling through syllables may be more effective than letters and sounds
The words Gavin naturally uses in speech tend to have too many letters for the memory span of this 'think faster' pupil. He uses polysyllabic words like 'elephant' or 'photosynthesis' appropriately in speech but struggles with the spelling. The problem will be accentuated if word building is done on a letter by letter basis. The memory span and working memory demands may be too great. But these words are easily chunked into syllables, significantly reducing memory demands.

So the principle, 'If he can clap it he can spell it' will work, once Gavin has a degree of grapheme/phoneme correspondence. He also does not need to be automatic on the alphabet arc for syllables to work as the strong visual element reinforces the auditory.

Gavin is finding the following approach effective for regular polysyllabic words like 'photosynthesis'.

1. Hand under chin – 'say it and chin it' – how many times does your jaw move?
2. Check and confirm by 'Say and clap'
3. Write the word across the full width of a strip of A4 paper and separate the syllables with forward slashes – pho / to / syn / the / sis
4. Tear the word into its beats and jumble up the pieces

3. Gavin should not always try to decode unknown words as an initial strategy
Gavin definitely thinks faster than he reads and his comprehension scores are always better than his reading accuracy. This is because he is managing to use his reasoning skills to fill in the gaps. Gavin needs a metacognitive menu of word attack strategies, with decoding/ sounding out being only one of many.

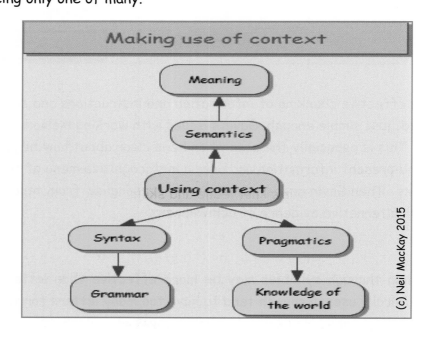

One strategy to be considered is, "If in doubt leave it out and read on to the next full stop". This strategy, involving the application of context, pragmatics and semantics in conjunction with higher order thinking skills to attack unknown words, comes at a price, it may be a bit unreliable at times.

The trade-off is that comprehension often improves because the flow of reading is not interrupted by the need to stop and sound out. When this approach does not work, sounding out is an essential tool which must be taught to mastery. But offering Gavin a menu of approaches and opportunities to try out can only be helpful, and can also be true for other pupils without a label who think faster than they read.

4. At present alternative evidence of achievement is the most accurate indicator of achievement for Gavin

Gavin's class teacher challenged him to "show me what you know about what you would see if you flew over a volcanic eruption, but you can't use sentences or paragraphs". Normally Gavin would have struggled to demonstrate his understanding conventionally but, when given permission to personalise his work, he was able to demonstrate not only his understanding, but also that he had been taught effectively.

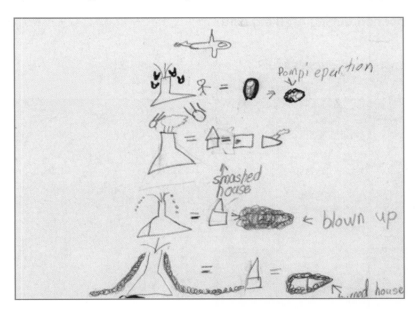

A challenge for schools wishing to optimise the impact of the pupil premium is to revisit their assessment policies to ensure that a range of evidence is required. Tracking Gavin's scores against the assessment task instead of just looking at raw scores may show that it is the task that is the barrier, rather than Gavin's knowledge and skills. Gavin's teacher used to dismiss alternative evidence because "you can't do that in SATS".

She now appreciates that mind-maps, story-boards, flow-charts, etc. are powerful springboards for writing, once they have been explicitly taught. Gavin is also being taught how to 'talk for writing' and can add value to a plan by talking it through, adding the high tariff connectives and 'wow' words that are much easier to remember and use when working from a plan.

5. Differentiation by outcome is not lazy teaching. Rather it is a cornerstone of personalisation

Gavin's basic skill levels tended to define the sorts of tasks he was asked to do, one consequence being that he was often under stretched intellectually. He became frustrated when he compared what he was being asked to do with a more challenging task on another tables.

"He could think it, he just couldn't ink it"

A Total Teaching approach is to ensure that Gavin be explicitly taught to use mind-maps, story-boards, flow-charts and bullet-points to mastery. Now he can work in his comfort zones and be celebrated for his differences/preferences. But it is also important to add the rigour of 'forced choice' to challenge Gavin to work in less preferred ways and to develop his range of skills. These evidence samples show a range of responses to the questions:

"What happened during a Viking raid?"
   and
"Why were they so successful?"

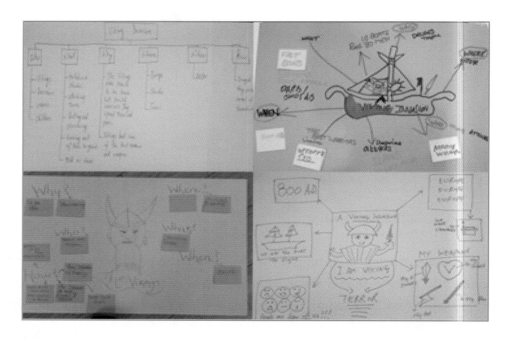

While each has its merits and some are better than others, they all represent valid outcomes in terms of knowledge and skills.

The teacher accepted Gavin's annotated drawing of the Viking ship for marking, managed to resist the temptation to ask him to write it up, and celebrated his achievement. During the formal assessment, Gavin was reminded of his Viking ship and advised to make a quick sketch and then write it up. He visualised his picture and labels, used it as the framework for writing while 'talking for writing' in his head.

A classroom provision map – the ultimate Total Teaching solution?

Name	Differ-entiated Planning	Differ-entiated Outputs	Marked Alternative Evidence of Achievem't	Enhanced Visual/ Auditory Inputs	Illus. Dictionary	Simplified Language	Slower Pace	Writing Frames	Access to computer	In-class support	Focus group work with support

What a result for Total Teaching!

This classroom provision map sets out the teacher's core offer to stuck pupils like Gavin. It is by no means comprehensive in terms of what should/could be available but it is a good start. In an interesting change of roles, one of the TAs has agreed to supervise the whole class group activities, enabling focussed group work to take place with the class teacher, this is proving particularly effective for Gavin.

Gavin is now a happy young man who looks forward to going to school because he knows that he will be successful at some time in every lesson. The Total Teaching fine tuning enables him to participate and deliver in ability appropriate activities and his class teacher is using the strategies to help more and more individuals without always needing to give individual help.

References

1. **LUCID LASS**, See www.lucid-research.com

2. **Tracy Packiam Alloway and Ross Alloway, Understanding Working Memory** Sage Publications, 2015

3. **Jungle Memory,** See www.junglememory.com

Chapter 12

Total Teaching:
an international perspective

At around 08.30 in the UK, Australia, Hong Kong, New Zealand, USA and beyond, students are dragging their way to school in the certain knowledge that, for yet another day, they will struggle to learn in the way they are being taught.

Although many of these students do not have formal labels, many will have similar types of needs to those already assessed as being Dyslexic, Dyspraxic, ASD or ADHD. The numbers are significant, for example, Professor Sally Shaywitz[1] is now suggesting that as many as 15-20% of students have Dyslexic type needs. Every teacher recognises students who struggle to 'get it out of their heads and on to paper', to maintain their focus, cope with change or with aspects of organisation and/or coordination, despite age or ability appropriate skills in other areas

Interestingly the picture in Australia, Europe, Hong Kong and New Zealand is very similar in a number of ways. Until recently in the UK and currently in many other countries, there has been a view among teachers that, 'until we get a label for these students, we cannot do anything'. Now the UK inspection process requires schools to put support in place while the assessment process is taking place on the assumption that a label will be forthcoming. Also on the grounds that nothing will be lost if the assessment does not result in an official label.

In reality, the needs of more and more students will have to be met from within a school's own resources, something which is being mirrored in other countries. In South Australia, for example, the DECD (Department for Education and Child Development) states that, in 2013, it provided "$12.441M for Learning Difficulties.... through the school's Resource Entitlement Statement and the school makes a decision on how this funding is used."

So, in South Australia there is funding but it is not ring-fenced, nor does there appear to be too much accountability for the way the money is spent. This pattern of funding without due accountability is repeated in many countries. In the UK however, there has been significant research into the impact of funding through the 'pupil premium', this significant sum of money each student in receipt of a free school meal brings into school. Some schools in deprived areas (low SEES/low decile schools) receive huge sums of money each year and the impact of their spending on student achievement has been monitored and researched by the Sutton Trust[2].

UK schools are now being required to demonstrate how their use of the pupil premium funding has impacted on the achievement of vulnerable groups which, in turn, is leading to more rigorous and accountable approaches.

OFSTED is also challenging schools to ensure that there are:

> *"no barriers to every child achieving (and an) even greater obligation*
> *to plan lessons for low levels of prior attainment."*

While I would not wish the UK's punitive inspection regime on other countries there is no doubt that what gets inspected gets done and there is, for the moment at least, rare accord in the language of Government and OFSTED in terms of all teachers being responsible for the progress of all students in a class. This can only benefit vulnerable groups in the future. The Education Board of Hong Kong (EDB) uses similar rhetoric but anecdotal evidence suggests that the impact is very varied across the three school bands although schools and local psychologists make valiant efforts to get students assessed in order to trigger the release of ring fenced funding. The situation is different in New Zealand and Australia where securing an official label of educational need is dependent upon parental ability to afford a private assessment.

In New Zealand in particular this is leading to worrying disparities between the number of students gaining accommodations for National Standards (the New Zealand version of the UK's SATs and Australia's NAPLAN) and public exams from fee paying schools and those in government/state/public schools. Recent figures from New Zealand collated by the Dyslexia Foundation of New Zealand (DFNZ) show that no students from a decile 1 school received accommodations, presumably because neither school nor parents could afford to put students through the appropriate assessments. Meanwhile the high status, fee paying school next door was successful in gaining exam accommodations for a significant percentage of students. This suggests that, in New Zealand at least, a child cannot be Dyslexic unless parents can afford a private assessment. There is a similar situation in Australia and Hong Kong, and increasingly in the UK, where parents are paying for the sort of specialist support that, in the UK at least, was once the right of all children.

Central government ministries and departments of education are well aware of the problems and are trying extremely hard to redress the situation, seeing the immediate solution to be changes in the way vulnerable students are taught in the unsupported classroom. In New Zealand, for example, the current focus is on raising the achievement of 'priority learners', those who traditionally do less well in school and there are initiatives with a similar focus in the UK, Hong Kong and Australia.

There is a touching faith, particularly in the UK and USA, that the solution lies in changes to teacher training. This ignores several realities. University schools of education are extremely difficult to move forward once courses have been set in the stone of academic validation.

Anecdotal evidence from young teachers suggests that few lecturers have recent teaching experience and so are preparing students to teach in schools and classrooms that no longer exist. Apparently young teachers are still being advised not to smile for the first term and, even if university courses were to be changed tomorrow it would take years before the young teachers were in a position to effect whole school change.

Changing the way teachers are trained is an obvious long term and important step, but focussing efforts on this condemns yet more generations of vulnerable students to failure. So we need a quick fix, in fact a whole range of quick fixes that all teachers can implement immediately, as and when dictated by a student's learning needs. The initial quick fix is for all teachers to embrace the challenge of becoming Total Teachers. Basically to acquire 'just enough' of the knowledge, skills and insights of special needs specialists so that they can take front line action when a student without a label, but with clearly identifiable needs, fails to make progress.

Or, to put it another way, Total Teaching kicks in when class teaching is failing to have 'enough impact' on achievement. This book is about supporting very busy and extremely hard working teachers to do just that. To notice vulnerable students; to have an appropriate level of awareness to identify the next steps across a range of learning needs that would, in another financial and political climate, have triggered 'pull out' interventions and to adjust the teaching and learning environment accordingly. This is not about major changes but more about fine tuning or tweaking current great practice to be even more inclusive and to help more and more individuals without always needing to give individual help.

International Total Teaching Perspectives

In Australia, the Gonski Report[3] was initially very influential. There were posters about "Giving a Gonski" in every staffroom and, prior to a change of government, hopes were high that the report would lead to massive increases in funding. While there is much to be praised in Gonski the report has stalled, largely because of a naïve recommendation for smaller class sizes.

This recommendation is naïve because it is unaffordable in the current economic climate and actually contradicts research which indicates that, unless class sizes are massively reduced, the measure has little or no impact. Research from the Sutton Trust in the UK suggests that:

> "the benefits of reducing class sizes are not particularly large or clear, until class size is reduced to under 20 or even below 15."

Unfortunately, the rhetoric surrounding this aspect of the Report has obscured other very valuable and sensible recommendations.

Much of what Gonski is suggesting makes real sense at a time of cuts and squeezes because, once the focus moves away from class sizes, it is clear that the report is actually about very achievable and desirable changes in classroom practice. Gonski, possibly without realizing it, is actually advocating Total Teaching.

A cornerstone of the Report is the need for what Gonski calls 'early diagnosis'. I regret the use of pseudo-medical jargon in an educational setting but would definitely accept the need for all teachers to 'look for trouble' when students are stuck and to modify methods, materials, strategies, groupings and approaches in order to move them on.

In this context it would be appropriate to replace 'diagnosis' with the Total Teaching 'notice and adjust' response.   However it is difficult to argue against the fact that looking for trouble, in terms of identifying students who are not benefitting enough from their education, does allow for early identification and immediate classroom action.

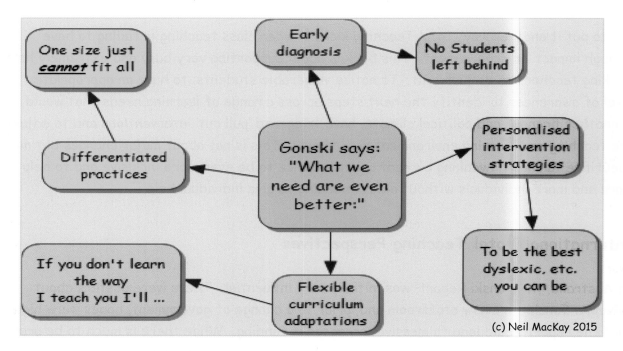

Gonski's four strands of recommended action are:

- early diagnosis/identification
- personalised intervention
- flexible adaptations
- differentiated practices

These are all eminently deliverable by class teachers and, when properly implemented, go a long way towards reducing the number of students requiring additional support, especially if teachers adopt the principles and approaches implicit within the Total Teaching model.

So elements of the Gonski Report are appropriate to include as part of an international model to develop the 'just enough' skillset.

Education in Australia is organised around the five states with each state seeking a unique educational personality within a common core. In 2014, Foundation to Year 10 Australian Curriculum is being implemented in all states and territories of Australia, to include learning areas, general capabilities and cross-curriculum priorities that support 21st century learning. The aim is for all young people to be supported to become "successful learners, confident and creative individuals, and active and informed citizens".

The document uses the phrase 'reasonable adjustments' to describe accommodations that balance the needs of students against the wider needs of the school community, which may offer a semantic route for some schools to deny their responsibilities across a range of learning needs. However, the school and college Principals I have worked with are determined that all students will achieve their potential, though many also recognise that this requires a general upskilling of teachers and teacher aides to remedy gaps between current student needs and levels of expertise developed during initial teacher training.

Dyslexia Aware Quality Mark

This is where the whole school professional development offered as part of the Dyslexia Aware Quality Mark is proving so successful in South Australia. The main focus is on enabling teachers to make reasonable adjustments across a range of learning needs, not just Dyslexia, as part of the 'notice and adjust' paradigm that underpins the training. Where these adjustments are translated into 'Personalised Learning' (something which is writ large in documentation relating to the Australian Curriculum), real opportunities exist to meet many more needs in the classroom rather than relying solely on 'pull out' support to plug gaps. This can easily be done in class when teachers have a higher level of all round awareness and training.

In Australia, this combination of house style underpinned by commonality is reflected in the publications produced by each State. South Australia has produced an excellent document called Teaching for Effective Learning[4] (TfEL) which is based around 4 domains. Domain 4, 'Personalise and Connect' is of particular significance to Total Teaching because it focusses on the need for personalisation to meet individual needs, one size fits all is definitely not the ethos that drives TfEL.

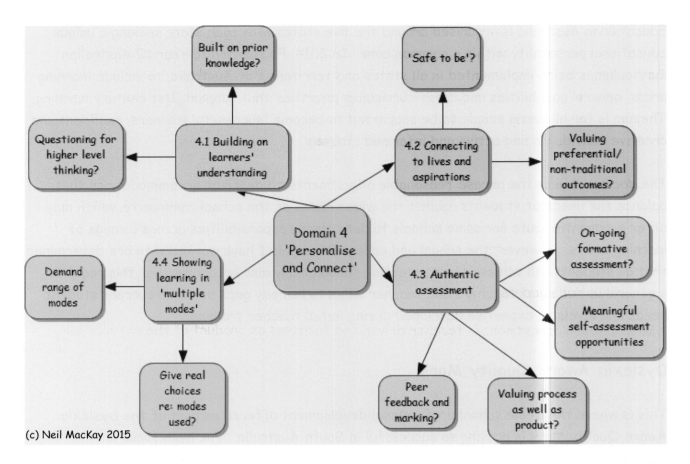

(c) Neil MacKay 2015

The approaches recommended in TfEL will support a range of learning needs through generic good practice rather than relying on outside or expert intervention. The needs of students without labels but who are currently facing barriers because of 'undiagnosed' learning needs will be well met in a learning environment which starts from where the child is, rather than some arbitrary notion of where s/he should be. While highlighting the attributes of an inclusive classroom, in a refreshing change from other official documents, TfEL also identifies classroom situations which will not be conducive to the desired outcomes.

The document makes it clear that the conditions necessary for inclusion cannot exist under the following circumstances:

4.1 While building on learners' understanding is a key principle which requires a complete understanding of students' prior attainment and learning. TfEL makes it clear that this will not work when teachers ignore prior learning and go for covering the curriculum at the expense of mastery.

4.2 Although attempts to connect to lives and aspirations are essential in order to contextualise learning and make it real for students from disparate backgrounds, experiences and aspirations these attempts will fail if, for example, teachers ignore and/or reject the current student preference for using technology, including iPads, tablets, mobile phones, blogs, web pages, eBooks and the growing 'bring your own device' movement.

This failure will be compounded if 'luddite' teachers only value and teach through traditional, print based literacies, only accepting for marking and levelling those traditional, usually print-based, forms of evidence of achievement. It is essential that schools avoid the temptation, often driven by politicians and 'Tiger Mums and Tiger Dads', to prepare children for a world that no longer exists – a classic example of this is requiring numerically challenged children to learn tables when giving them a calculator would be much more effective in terms of learning mathematical concepts.

> *4.3 Authentic assessment is as much about informing students as it is the teacher. When formative, on-going self-assessment is built into the teaching and learning process, students are always aware of where they are in relation to their learning goals, how close they are to achieving them and their next steps for success.*

However when assessment is teacher driven and focusses on product at the expense of process, vulnerable students may fail for up to a term before the next summative assessment flags up any issues. Of course books will have been marked during this time, but unhelpful marking practices, especially those giving feedback rather than advice which feeds forward to making the next piece more successful, compound the over-reliance of summative assessments. Failing to engage students in the assessment process takes away any sense of ownership of success or failure as assessment becomes something 'done to' students rather than with their active participation.

> *4.4 Sharing learning in multiple modes is about using assessment for learning and alternative evidence of achievement to make learning visible as part of on-going assessment.*

It is also concerned with demanding a range of evidence of learning, some of which will be outside a student's zone of comfort and pushing into an individual's Zone of Proximal Development (ZPD). This is loosely the difference between what a student can do with support or maybe a scaffold or framework, and what they can do unaided. Tracking marks across a range of evidence is a sure way for a Total Teacher to identify quick thinking, slow reading students who struggle to show what they know traditionally but who do so effectively through alternative evidence and assessment for learning techniques.

For example, students for whom English is a second or additional language (ESL/EAL) may struggle to write at length to demonstrate their learning but may do so very effectively in multiple modes, maybe by labelling a diagram or completing a framework. So this is as much to do with teachers assessing the impact of their teaching as it is with student outcomes. However, when written communication predominates and teachers are reluctant to set deliberately ambitious targets for fear of adverse reactions many students will struggle to make their learning visible and others will coast.

In a nutshell TfEL is driving assessment for learning to identify prior levels of knowledge, learning and attainment. The imperative to build on prior learning carries with it an obligation to teach the students rather than the lesson as planned. Recognising the importance of IT driven literacies and placing them alongside traditional print based ones supports students to take their place in the world as it is now and will become, also enabling schools to respond to and anticipate future challenges.

This determination to secure a range of evidence of achievement manifests in a commitment to formative assessment in order to engage students in their learning. It also informs lesson planning and delivery as Total Teachers respond to the natural ebb and flow of understanding, skill acquisition and concept development during a lesson. The whole process is held together by subtle blends of personalised tasks offering a combination of free choice, forced choice and no choice, enabling students to operate in their zones of proximal development in safety and security.

While the principle of Total Teaching, as exemplified by TfEL, seems to be alive and well in South Australia as well as in other States, the challenge for Principals and Leadership Teams is to find ways to make best practice common practice, in fact, to embrace the philosophy and principles of Total Teaching.

In New Zealand there is an emphasis on raising the achievement of priority learners[5], defined by the Education Review Office (ERO) as

> "groups of students who have been identified as historically
> not experiencing success in the New Zealand schooling system."

This group includes Maori and Pacifica learners as well as those from low socio-economic groups and students with special educational needs. A range of measures has been implemented over the years and there is a current focus on assessment for learning. The language is similar to TfEL and emphasises the importance of high expectations, involving students in the learning process and employing a flexible range of techniques to respond to the expectation that every student can improve. The documentation also references John Hattie's[4] 'visible learning' to confirm the importance of the student thinking process being made visible to the teacher.

I have had the opportunity to share the principles behind Total Teaching in workshops across New Zealand and the response has been encouraging. However conversations with teachers indicate that very mixed messages are coming from Principals and Leadership teams regarding the viability and appropriateness of alternative, non-traditional forms of assessment.

Interestingly there are similar concerns among leaders in New Zealand and the UK. New Zealand introduced national testing in the form of National Standards several years ago and the path to centralised assessment has not been smooth. This is principly due to the combination of a well-established culture of self-managing schools accountable mainly to the Board of Trustees and clumsy implementation by the Ministry of Education.

Without becoming involved in the debate on the educational validity of high stakes testing there is a very clear and positive message coming from the Ministry and the Education Review Office (ERO) regarding appropriate forms of assessment – all of which are a good fit with the Total Teaching model and which also resonate with TfEL in Australia.

Teachers are urged to use a range of assessment approaches including:

- conversations about learning between teachers and students
- taking simple mental notes during observation
- students assessing themselves and each other
- detailed analysis of student work
- using a range of formal assessment tools

These types of assessments will support priority learners to show what they know despite language skills and/or basic skills which are not currently fit for purpose. They will also inform teachers very accurately about the impact of teaching on learning, enabling lessons to be personalised in order to meet individual needs.

ERO is promoting 'responsive schooling', a helpful phrase which encompasses, among other things, individualised learning and support given to students and careful tracking and monitoring of achievement, with the whole process being driven by robust review and improvement of teaching and support initiatives. Responsive pedagogy is at the heart of Total Teaching and the teachers I have worked with in North and South Island are committed to flexible ways of promoting and assessing learning.

While there seems to be continuing doubt among some teachers about the validity of informal assessments when it comes to levelling students for National Standards, the Ministry has given very clear 'permission' for a range of evidence to be used as the basis for the Overall Teacher Judgement (OTJ), including a variety of evidence teachers already collect, such as the student's work, peer and self-assessment, everyday classroom observation, and assessment activities (both formal and informal).

In Hong Kong the Education Board (EDB) has been driving the need for more responsive and flexible approaches to learning needs through its website and also through a commitment to professional development. Hong Kong teachers in Government schools work incredibly hard to take learning forward, but many struggle with the concept of accommodations as a way of responding to specific learning needs.

There is a very strong, almost culturally driven view, that it is somehow 'unfair' to give one student extra time or permission to do a mind-map instead of an essay. It is felt that accommodations somehow make things easier for that student, so all students should be in the same position. This view, which is contrary to the official view put forward by the EDB, actually bubbles under the surface among teachers, young and old, in many countries, who fail to appreciate that interventions and accommodations do no more than level the playing field for some rather than giving unfair advantage.

There is a thriving international school community in Hong Kong, with pupils from many different countries, including a very strong presence from the English Schools Foundation (ESF). Most international schools, with the possible exception of ESF, seem to have major problems recognising and responding to students who learn differently and need slightly personalised teaching. The defence usually centres around the pressure to get students through exams, but it is interesting to note that in Dubai, another international educational hothouse, GEMS International Schools have very well developed processes and facilities to identify and meet the needs of vulnerable students and seem able to do this without compromising academic excellence.

However, the language necessary to drive Total Teaching in Hong Kong is evident in directives and documentation coming from EDB. Just as in other countries there is a commitment to assessment for learning which, if it is to be realised, requires teachers to learn and adopt the skills of Total Teaching. The importance of a range of formative assessments is emphasised, together with the need for peer collaboration. EDB also makes it clear that class and subject teachers are responsible for the learning of all students and encourages them to "look for alternatives to individual support, e.g. through the planning of lessons, group teaching, etc."

In the UK three strands came together in 2014 to make it essential that all class and subject teachers develop those 'just enough' skills of the Total Teacher. There is a new National Curriculum, a new Code of Practice for students with Special Educational Needs (SEN) and a new Framework for Inspections from the Office for Standards in Education (OFSTED). All three combine to demand more and more of teachers in a climate of less and less funding, resources and support.

The OFSTED report "Inclusion: does it matter where children are taught"[6] arguably began the debate in 2006. This is an important report which observed that:

1. High quality, specialist teachers and a commitment by leaders to create opportunities to include all pupils were the keys to success

2. Pupils in mainstream schools where support from teaching assistants was the main type of provision were less likely to make good academic progress than those who had access to specialist teaching in those schools.

Unfortunately, since publication of the Report funding to Local Authorities has been cut year on year, resulting in fewer and fewer specialist teachers being employed in schools. Initially schools tried using teaching assistants to plug the gaps, despite the concerns raised in point 2 above. But even this provision is being squeezed as schools try to meet more and more needs with less and less funding. There is a perception among many teachers in the UK that they are increasingly being left without support, despite growing pressure to raise the achievement of vulnerable groups.

The debate began to simmer in 2010 following a report by Janet Thompson, HMI, which stated that 25% of the 1.7 million pupils in England with SEN would not be so labelled if schools focussed more on teaching for all children. In a powerful statement, she observed that it was time to:

> "stop identifying students as having SEN when they simply needed better teaching".

I have used this challenging quote in my whole school training and consultancy work with thousands of teachers since 2011 and it is interesting to note that, while teaching unions found the statement 'insulting and wrong', a majority of teachers on my courses agreed with it in principle and generally considered it to be fair comment. Although almost everyone also remarked on how hard it was to meet the needs of increasing numbers of vulnerable students with decreasing support.

The statement has been refined and was summarised by the then Secretary of State for Education, Michael Gove, in a speech to the National College of Leaders and Teachers[7]:

> "Lessons should be planned to ensure that there are no barriers to every pupil achieving. In many cases, such planning will mean that these pupils will be able to study the full national curriculum".

This is echoed in the Code of Practice:

- Class teachers are responsible and accountable for progress and development – regardless of the level of other support
- Quality first teaching is the benchmark – additional support/intervention cannot compensate for lack of this

The final strand is the National Curriculum Framework in England[8], 2013. This document outlines the next statutory National Curriculum, which has a clear statement on inclusion and a very strong emphasis on developing the basics of literacy and numeracy through thematic approaches to the programmes of study. This is especially important as the time available for the discrete teaching of literacy and numeracy has been reduced in an attempt to re-create a broad and balanced curriculum. In the UK many schools have responded to the pressure of high stakes national testing (SATs) and the subsequent publication of league tables by narrowing the curriculum to spend more time on what is being assessed.

One interesting outcome from changes in the UK has been a gradual move away from looking at the level of support as a starting point to beginning with a conversation about desired outcomes, in other words to begin with where the student needs to be and then to look at how to get there. The problem with taking support as a starting point is that it invariably becomes bogged down in assessment, cost and unhelpfully doctrinal arguments about in-class support versus withdrawal/pullout. Starting with outcomes immediately opens up a range of options, from more personalised class teaching at one end to 'pull out' support at the other with a whole range and combination of approaches in between. Built in to this process is regular and thorough assessment of the impact of what is happening to the student.

When the impact is not what teacher, parents and students are expecting, when, for example, data or marking shows that the gap between ability and performance is not closing, a focus on outcomes allows a menu of available approaches, including pull out support, to kick in as required. This is in contrast to what happens when the initial focus is on support, especially when it follows a private report from an Educational Psychologist which stipulates 20 hours of 1:1 per week! Most of us have seen absurd support recommendations in our time and know the damage they can do to relations with parents who are desperately worried about their child and, having paid good money for an assessment, find it hard to accept that the recommendations may not always be in the best interests of their child.

The best place to start looking at setting and achieving outcomes has to be the classroom. Even when a vulnerable student receives out of class support, s/he will spend most of the time in class, usually being taught by a teacher who is unlikely to have a specialist qualification in special educational needs. However if the teacher is a Total Teacher s/he will notice that current provision is not having enough impact and have just enough of the skills and awareness of a specialist to adjust the methods, materials, approaches, groupings, differentiation, etc. accordingly.

This fine tuning will work for many students currently in receipt of 'support' which is often inefficient, especially when it is 1:1, and of limited impact, but has been put in place at the insistence of concerned parents. When this still does not have enough impact the best schools have a continuum of measures available which become increasingly personalised.

Total Teaching schools also enable students to access the more specific intervention without waiting for assessments. If the students need it and the school can deliver, they get it quickly and efficiently. Waiting for the results of an assessment and an official label before intervening is inefficient and arguably unprofessional because it condemns a student to potentially months of unfulfilled needs while a bureaucratic process grinds its way along.

The best advice would seem to be that, if in doubt as to the nature of a students learning needs, basically "Is it Dyslexia, ADHD, etc.?" Assume it is and take appropriate classroom action which can become progressively more personalised until it reaches a level at which desired outcomes are being achieved.

References:

1. **Sally E. Shaywitz,** *Overcoming Dyslexia*
   Random House, USA, 2005

2. **Sutton Trust, Education Endowment Foundation**
   NFER TEacher Voice Omnibus Survey 2014
   http://www.suttontrust.com/newsarchive/nearly-1-4-teachers-think-pupil-premium-funds-may-targeted-poorest-students-sutton-trust-poll

3. **David Gonski, Review of Funding for Schooling**
   http://pandora.nla.gov.au/pan/132421/20131129-1201/Review-of-Funding-for-Schooling-Final-Report.pdf

4. **South Australian Teaching for Effective Learning Framework**
   http://www.learningtolearn.sa.edu.au/tfel/pages/tfelresources/satfelframeworkguide/?reFlag=1

5. **Ministry of Education, New Zealand, Focus on Priority Learners**
   http://www.minedu.govt.nz/theMinistry/EducationInitiatives/InvestingInEducationalSuccess/Report/Part2/FoundationElements/Focus.aspx

6. **OFSTED,** Inclusion: does it matter where children are taught
   HMI 2535, July 2006 (Download available)

7. **National College of Leaders Conference 2013, Seizing Success**
   http://www.eteachblog.com/michael-gove-at-the-national-college-of-leaders-conference-seizing-success/

8. **Department for Education, National Curriculum in England: framework for key stages 1 to 4,** Sept 2013
   https://www.gov.uk/government/publications/national-curriculum-in-england-framework-for-key-stages-1-to-4